CALVIN
and the
BIBLICAL
LANGUAGES

CALVIN
and the
BIBLICAL LANGUAGES

John D. Currid

MENTOR

To all my Hebrew Students

Copyright © John D. Currid 2006

ISBN 1-84550-212-4
ISBN 978-1-84550-212-6

Published in 2006
by
Christian Focus Publications, Geanies House,
Fearn, Ross-shire, IV20 1TW, Scotland.

www.christianfocus.com

Cover design by Danie Van Straaten

Printed and bound by
Bell & Bain, Glasgow

All rights reserved. No part of this publication may be reproduced, stored in a retrieval system, or transmitted, in any form, by any means, electronic, mechanical, photocopying, recording or otherwise without the prior permission of the publisher or a license permitting restricted copying. In the U.K. such licenses are issued by the Copyright Licensing Agency, 90 Tottenham Court Road, London W1P 9HE.

Contents

A Brief Time-Line of John Calvin's Life 7

Chapter One
The Christian Hercules 9

Chapter Two
The Exegetical Preacher 21

Chapter Three
King of Commentators 31

Chapter Four
This Most Faithful Interpreter 45

Chapter Five
The Academy 51

Chapter Six
That Singular Instrument of God 65

Postscript
A Plea 79

Appendix
A Sermon of John Calvin on Deuteronomy 16:1-4 85

A Brief Time-Line of John Calvin's Life

1509	Born in Noyon, France (July 10)
1523–1527	Student at College de Montaigu, Paris
1528–1533	Law Studies at Orléans and Bourges Intermittent Study in Paris
1534	Year of Wandering
1535–1536	Calvin in Basel
1536	*Institutes of the Christian Religion* Published
1536–1538	First Stay in Geneva
1538	Calvin and Farel Expelled from Geneva
1538–1541	Calvin in Strassburg Romans Commentary Published (1540) Calvin Marries Idelette de Bure (1540)
1541	Returns to Geneva *Ecclesiastical Ordinances* Approved in Geneva
1549	Calvin's Wife Idelette de Bure Dies
1553	Trial and Execution of Michael Servetus in Geneva
1559	Establishment of the Geneva Academy
1564	Calvin Dies (May 27)

Chapter One

The Christian Hercules

The *realia*

Theodore Beza once commented regarding John Calvin that he 'was a kind of Christian Hercules who subdued many ministers by the mightiest of all clubs, the Word of God. As many adversaries as Satan stirred up against him, so many trophies did the Lord bestow upon his servant.'[1] Numerous works have appeared over the years treating John Calvin's use of this 'club', that is, his hermeneutics or exegetical principles.[2] To put it simply, Calvin desired to get at the real meaning (the *realia*) of the biblical text. Hunter puts it this way: 'fidelity to the meaning of the original was his first principle.'[3]

Prior to the Reformation, this principle of determining the original meaning of a text as the basis of interpretation

---

1 Quoted by J. C. Bowman, 'Calvin as a Preacher,' *Reformed Church Review* 13 (1909):253.

2 See, in particular, D. L. Puckett, *John Calvin's Exegesis of the Old Testament* (Louisville: Westminster/John Knox Press, 1995); and the articles by H. Kraus, T. H. L. Parker, and J. L. M. Haire in R. C. Gamble, *Calvin and Hermeneutics* (New York: Garland, 1992).

3 A. M. Hunter, 'Calvin as a Preacher,' *Expository Times* 30, 12 (1919):563.

(known today as grammatical-historical exegesis) was not common.[4] Although elements of it were found in movements like the Antiochene School, which includes such scholars as Theodore of Mopsuestia (350–428; he was called 'the Exegete') and John Chrysostom (344–407), the reality is that it was a rare hermeneutical position.[5] The clearly dominant position before the Reformation was allegory. During the Patristic period, the Alexandrian School held interpretive sway in the church of the day, and the allegorical method was its centerpiece. Origen (185–254) did more exegetical work than anyone prior to the Reformation, and his work was dominated by allegory. He said he sought 'to discover in every expression the hidden splendor of the doctrines veiled in common and unattractive phraseology'.[6] Origen held to a trichotomy of interpretation: as there is a Trinity and there are three parts to every person (body, soul, and spirit), thus there are three senses to every text of Scripture. These three meanings are literal, allegorical, and moral.

One example from Origen will suffice to demonstrate his interpretive methodology of the Bible. In Genesis 24, we read that Rebekah comes to draw water from the well, and there she meets the servant of Abraham. Origen interpreted this episode to mean that each believer must come daily to the wells of Scripture in order to meet with Christ.[7]

Even Augustine (354–430), the great defender of the orthodox faith, was enamored with allegory as a proper means of exegesis. He was obviously deficient in both Hebrew and Greek, and he believed that the Old Latin translation was

---

[4] For a good survey of pre-Reformation hermeneutics, see D. McCartney and C. Clayton, *Let the Reader Understand: A Guide to Interpreting and Applying the Bible* (Phillipsburg, NJ: Presbyterian and Reformed, 2002, 2nd ed.).

[5] For a recent and important study of Chrysostom, see J. N. D. Kelly, *Golden Mouth: The Story of John Chrysostom: Ascetic, Preacher, Bishop* (Grand Rapids: Baker, 1998).

[6] *De principiis*, 4.1.7.

[7] F. W. Farrar, *History of Interpretation* (Grand Rapids: Baker reprint, 1979), p. 199.

singularly inspired. Augustine's exegetical principles are enumerated in his work *On Christian Doctrine*. In that work it is clear that he held the literal and historical sense of a biblical passage in high regard; yet, it is not enough. The Bible has more than one meaning, and the allegorical method is a way of clarifying the obscure.

During the Middle Ages, most biblical study was isolated in monasteries. Strident allegory was the dominant interpretive method of the time. A fourfold sense to Scripture was commonplace: literal, allegoric, moral, and mystical. One of the leading lights was Hugh of St. Victor (1096–1141). He wrote a book titled *On the Sacraments of the Christian Faith*, and it served as an introduction to the allegorical study of the Old Testament. For example, his understanding of the throne room scene in Isaiah 6 reeks of allegory. He said that the seraphim, who are angelic creatures surrounding God's throne, actually represent the sacred Scriptures. The three pairs of wings on each creature symbolically picture a proper interpretive method: literal, allegoric, and moral![8]

Thomas Aquinas was one of the most profound thinkers and theologians that the Middle Ages produced. He was, however, a weak exegete. When interpreting Scripture, Aquinas gave meager explanations of the literal sense of a text. His hermeneutics was imbued with the fourfold sense of Scripture. Overwhelming and long-winded arguments in addition to speculative discussions were rampant (e.g., when looking at Job he goes on relentlessly about good angels in contrast to bad angels). He accepted many tasteless and empty allegories. For instance, when the text says that John the Baptist ate wild honey and locusts, this means that John's preaching to the crowds was sweet like honey, but short of flight like locusts.

In contrast, the Reformation emphasized a literal interpretation of the text; Christian doctrine must be based

---

8 For further study of this period, see H. de Lubac, *Medieval Exegesis* (Grand Rapids: Eerdmans, 1998).

on the original and literal intent of the authors of Scripture. There is little or no room for allegory. Calvin called allegory a contrivance of Satan and merely a bunch of monkey tricks! Hand in hand with the reformational principle of grammatical-historical exegesis was the conviction that at the heart of interpretation are the biblical languages. The exegetical task 'can be accomplished only through a solid knowledge of the Greek and Hebrew languages'.[9] In reality, while much has been written about Calvin's exposition of Scripture, little has been penned regarding his knowledge and use of these languages in his life's work and ministry.[10] That is the purpose and subject of this book, and I hope this work will help promote further study of this topic.

King of the commentators
In a well-known statement, the 17th century French Catholic cleric Richard Simon (1638–1712) claimed that John Calvin was basically ignorant of the Hebrew language of the Old Testament.[11] In fact, he 'went so far as to say that Calvin knew little more than the characters of the Hebrew alphabet'.[12] Others argue that this accusation was false and that it was an aspersion on the academic character of Calvin. These proponents say that, in reality, Calvin had a thorough knowledge of the biblical languages, and he was fully competent in their use to perform exegesis of a biblical text. A. M. Hunter remarks about Calvin's skill in the original languages:

> ... suffice it to say that in spite of depreciative assertions, an impartial student of his commentaries cannot but admit that he was more than adequately equipped to deal authoritatively with

---

9 H. Kraus, 'Calvin's Exegetical Principles,' *Interpretation* 31 (1977):14.
10 For introductory work on the subject, see J. D. Currid, 'Calvin as Hebraist: Guarding the Sacred Deposit,' *Reformed Theological Review* 63 (2004):61-71.
11 R. Simon, *Histoire critique du Vieux testament* (Rotterdam, 1685), p. 435.
12 W. McKane, 'Calvin as an Old Testament Commentator,' in R. Gamble, ed. *Calvin and Hermeneutics* (New York: Garland, 1992), p. 250.

the originals of both Old Testament and New Testament.[13]

Who is right? Was John Calvin a good exegete who relied on a masterful knowledge of biblical languages or not? The truth of the matter is that most 'recent scholars have agreed that, for his time, Calvin was a distinguished textual scholar. Proficient in all three languages ...' – Hebrew, Greek, and Latin.[14] Such a view of Calvin's linguistic abilities has been around for a long time. In 1892, Philip Schaff made the observation that 'Calvin, besides being a master of Latin and French, had a very good knowledge of the languages of the Bible.'[15] The biblical languages were foundational to Calvin's exegetical prowess. Diestel said that Calvin was 'the creator of genuine exegesis'; Reuss, who was the chief editor of Calvin's works, said that Calvin was without question 'the greatest exegete of the sixteenth century'; and Schaff called him the 'king of the commentators'.[16] Calvin himself had the conviction of the essential importance of the biblical languages. He said, 'we cannot understand the teaching of God unless we know his styles and languages.'[17] The reality of the issue is summed up by Fuhrmann who says that a '*primary* merit of Calvin is to be a *philologist*'.[18]

Calvin learns Hebrew

There is quite a debate in Calvin scholarship regarding when and where Calvin first began the study of biblical Hebrew.

---

13 A. M. Hunter, 'The Erudition of John Calvin,' *Evangelical Quarterly* 18 (1946):203.

14 W. J. Bouwsma, *John Calvin: A Sixteenth Century Portrait* (New York: Oxford University Press, 1988), p. 117.

15 P. Schaff, 'Calvin as a Commentator,' *The Presbyterian and Reformed Review* 3 (1892):464.

16 G. Johnson, 'Calvinism and Interpretation,' *Evangelical Quarterly* 4 (1932):170-71.

17 *Opera* 47:465.

18 P. T. Fuhrmann, 'Calvin, Expositor of Scripture,' *Interpretation* 6.2 (April 1952):197.

Theodore Beza, who was rector of the Academy at Geneva and held its Greek chair, wrote a biography of Calvin that claimed the Reformer learned Hebrew in the city of Basel in 1534. He said about Calvin in those early days:

> There he lived on intimate terms with those two distinguished men, Simon Grynaeus and Wolfgang Capito, and devoted himself to the study of Hebrew.[19]

I believe this statement by Beza has often been misunderstood. In it, he nowhere alleges that Basel was the first place that Calvin studied Hebrew, but only that he 'devoted himself' to it there. The reality is that Calvin probably began his Hebrew studies in 1531, at the ripe age of twenty-two, when he was a student in Paris. As far as we can tell, this was approximately the time of his conversion to Christianity.[20]

Two years earlier, Francis I had founded a trilingual college that later came to be known as the great Collège de France. At the heart of the academic institution, the king had established several professorships for teaching Latin, Greek, and Hebrew. 'It was a great step in a new direction. Not many years before he would have been ridiculed for it by the Sorbonne; perhaps he was now. But the king selected the best professors whom he could obtain: Danes taught Greek, Vatable taught Hebrew.'[21] Calvin enrolled in the Collège de France, and almost certainly began his Hebrew studies under the renowned François Vatable (d. 1547), who was arguably the greatest Hebraist of his day.[22] Battles and Hugo remark: 'It is probable, though not altogether certain, that he also attended the lectures of Toussain and of his eminent Hebrew colleague, the celebrated

---

19 T. Beza, *The Life of John Calvin* (Edinburgh: Banner of Truth, 1982), p. 15.
20 See the discussion of Bouwsma, *John Calvin*, pp. 10-12.
21 W. Blackburn, *College Days of Calvin* (Philadelphia: Presbyterian Board of Publication, 1865), p. 139.
22 G. Lloyd Jones, *The Discovery of Hebrew in Tudor England: A Third Language* (Manchester: Manchester University Press, 1983), pp. 71-2.

Vatable.'²³ Vatable is rightly regarded as the restorer of Hebrew scholarship in France. Unfortunately, he wrote very little in his lifetime, and not much of even that has survived until today.

A few scholars argue that this incipient Hebrew study of Calvin was almost a curiosity, a mere 'dillettant'.²⁴ But the reality is that he began his studies in Hebrew in Paris in the year 1531, and then he did further in-depth work in Basel in 1535 and 1536, perhaps under the instruction of Sebastian Münster who was teaching Hebrew in the city at that time.²⁵ This was followed by even more learning of it in Strassburg during 1538 to 1541.²⁶

The founding of the Collège de France as a trilingual university reflected the shifting academic mood of the day in Europe. At this time there occurred an explosion of interest in Greek, Latin, and Hebrew studies.²⁷ Indeed, 'by the year 1550 one could find instruction in the Hebrew language at the majority of Western European universities.'²⁸ Yet, it was not

---

23 F. L. Battles and A. M. Hugo, *Calvin's Commentary on Seneca's de Clementia* (Leiden: Brill, 1969), p. 5.

24 Q. Breen, *John Calvin: A Study in French Humanism* (Hamden, CT: Archon Books, 1968), p. 64.

25 N. Lunn, 'Sebastian Münster – Hebraist of the Reformation,' *Banner of Truth* 490 (2004):8-14. Lunn comments, 'Though the Hebrew Old Testament together with the standard Jewish commentaries was available to him in the form of Blomberg's *Biblia Rabbinica* (1524-25), Calvin's knowledge of these latter writings was probably for the most part obtained indirectly through works such as Münster's *Hebraica Biblia*. We know for a fact that Calvin consulted Münster in the preparation of his commentaries' (p. 11). Münster was perhaps the most famous Hebraist of his age. He truly loved the Hebrew language, and he called it 'that holy and truly divine language'. See P. E. Lapide, *Hebrew in the Church: The Foundations of Jewish-Christian Dialogue* (Grand Rapids: Eerdmans, 1984), p. 53.

26 Puckett, *John Calvin's Exegesis of the Old Testament*, p. 58.

27 This was not a pure revival of Hebrew studies, but certainly a great expansion of interest in that language. Clearly, many scholars had a lofty opinion of Hebrew in the high Middle Ages. Indeed, 'it was the language of God, the first speech of mankind, and the medium of angels.' See A. C. Skinner, *Veritas Hebraica: Christian Attitudes Toward the Hebrew Language in the High Middle Ages* (Ph.D. diss., University of Denver, 1986), p. 323.

28 Ibid., p. 322.

without great opposition. In the academies of Europe in the first half of the sixteenth century 'there was widespread hostility to the renewed emphasis on classical antiquity and scorn for the paganism of the Greeks and Romans.'[29] Many academics of this period simply had contempt for the study of the biblical languages. This bias was specifically directed at the Collège de France in the early 1530s when a suit was brought by the Faculty of the Sorbonne against Vatable and other professors at the Collège de France enjoining them not to teach Hebrew and Greek. In a publication titled *Determinatio Facultatis* (April 30, 1530), the Sorbonne attacked those who believed that sound exegesis of the original texts helped to understand the Bible better.[30] Two propositions were made by the Faculty of the Sorbonne that clearly summarized their beliefs:

> First proposition: Holy Scripture cannot be understood properly without Greek, Hebrew, and other similar languages. Censura: this proposition is imprudent and scandalous. Second proposition: no preacher can explain the truth of an epistle or Gospel without the aforementioned languages. Censura: this proposition is false, impious, and prevents in a pernicious manner Christian people from hearing the Word of God. Moreover, the authors of these assertions are strongly suspected of *Lutheranism*.[31]

Battles and Hugo give further comment on this conflict:

> The very subjects, Greek and Hebrew, were revolutionary for those days (although cities like Alcala, Oxford, and Louvain had already taken the lead in this), and were regarded by the Paris theologians as dangerous in the extreme. The theologians smelt Lutheranism, and they did not hesitate to say so; but neither the

---

29 A. Katchen, *Christian Hebraists and Dutch Rabbis* (Cambridge, MA: Harvard University Press, 1984), p. 9.

30 A. Ganoczy, *The Young Calvin* (Philadelphia: The Westminster Press, 1987), p. 69.

31 A. Lefranc, *Histoire du Collège de France* (Paris: Hachette, 1893), p. 122.

King nor his chosen band of professors heeded such talk, and the institution grew apace, attracting students from far and wide.[32]

The fiercest hostility was against the study of Jewish literature and, especially, the language of Hebrew. Many of the European academicians believed that, 'even for biblical studies, Hebrew had no real value over the existing Latin.'[33] Even Erasmus, who did so much with the Koine Greek of the New Testament, questioned the true worth of much Hebrew study; he was afraid that so much emphasis on it may lead to a revival in Judaism.[34] He stated, for example:

> The restoration of Hebrew learning may give occasion to the revival of Judaism. This would be a plague as much opposed to the doctrine of Christ as anything that can happen.[35]

Despite such heated resistance, Calvin profited greatly from the new and rare advantage of learning biblical Hebrew. He made Hebrew, along with Greek and Latin, the very cornerstone of his studies and of his later preaching, teaching, and commentary work.[36]

---

32 Battles and Hugo, *Calvin's Commentary on Seneca's De Clementia*, p. 1.
33 Katchen, *Christian Hebraists*, p. 9.
34 J. C. Olin, ed. *Christian Humanism and the Reformation: Selected Writings of Erasmus* (New York: Harper and Row, 1965), p. 80. On this issue, Erasmus contradicted himself. For example, he wrote the following to Martin Dorp: 'How much better, instead of doing what they are doing – wounding others and being wounded, wasting their own time and that of others – to learn Greek or Hebrew, or at least Latin, which are so indispensable to the knowledge of Sacred Scripture that I think it extremely impudent for anyone ignoring them to usurp the name of theologian.'
35 J. Friedman, *The Most Ancient Testimony: Sixteenth-Century Christian-Hebraica in the Age of Renaissance Nostalgia* (Athens, OH: Ohio University Press, 1983), p. 178.
36 It is likely that Calvin was trained in Hebrew with Conrad Pellicanus' book *De modo legendi et intelligendi Hebraea* (1503). He also certainly used the Rabbinics of Kimchi, Ibn Ezra, and Rashi.

Calvin learns Greek

Although Calvin spent part of 1531 and 1532 studying in Paris, much of his academic work during these early years was spent in Orléans, a city which contained an important law university. Here, and at Bourges, Calvin worked on a law degree, and he became a *licencié* in the law. To the best of our knowledge, he studied at Orléans, off and on, from 1528 to 1533. Most important for our study is that at Orléans and Bourges Calvin came under the influence of Melchior Wolmar.

Wolmar was born in Rothwell in 1496. After serving as a schoolmaster for a number of years, 'in 1521 he went to Paris, where he studied Greek under Glareanus and Nicolas Béraud. In 1523 he published his annotations on two books of Homer's *Iliad*. Of one hundred candidates for the licentiate in arts at Paris he ranked number one.'[37] Wolmar was thoroughly and fervently reformational, and his views were considered dangerous in Paris. Thus, he moved to Orléans about 1527, no doubt because this city was more open to his religious opinions.

In Orléans, Wolmar took Calvin under his wing and 'initiated him into the rudiments of Greek'.[38] This initial Greek study was merely introductory, and it did not go beyond the bare essentials. Calvin admits this fact himself in the preface to his later *Commentary on Second Corinthians*. He dedicated that volume to Wolmar, and in the dedication he includes the following statement:

> But the main reason has been my recollection how, the first time my father sent me to study civil law, it was at your instigation and under your tuition that I also took up the study of Greek, of which you were at that time a most distinguished teacher. It was not your fault that I did not make greater progress.... Nevertheless

---

[37] F. L. Battles, *Interpreting John Calvin* (Grand Rapids: Baker Books, 1996), p. 58.
[38] Ganoczy, *The Young Calvin*, p. 68.

my indebtedness to you for this is still great for you gave me a good grounding in the rudiments of the language and that was a great help to me later on.[39]

Beza also studied Greek under Wolmar. In his biography of Calvin, Beza said about his Greek teacher:

> I have the greater pleasure in mentioning his name, because he was my own teacher, and the only one I had from boyhood up to youth. His learning, piety, and other virtues, together with his admirable abilities as a teacher of youth, cannot be sufficiently praised. On his suggestion, and with his assistance, Calvin learned Greek.[40]

Obviously Beza assigned too much credit to Wolmar in regard to Calvin's learning of biblical Greek. In reality, the most that can be said is that Wolmar merely laid the original foundation for Calvin's Greek study. But, most importantly, he did encourage and inspire Calvin to pick up and undertake that study.

In 1535 and 1536, Calvin resided in Basel. This city was 'a free center of humanist culture and a sure refuge for persecuted reformists'.[41] Here Calvin became increasingly convinced that the Bible was to be read and understood according to the original texts. At Basel, he greatly desired to develop his knowledge of Greek and to continue his Hebrew studies, and in that manner he hoped to deepen his familiarity with the sacred Scriptures.

Calvin met Simon Grynaeus at this time, and the latter proved to be of invaluable help for Calvin's instruction in Greek. Grynaeus had been professor of Greek at the University

---

39 John Calvin, *The Second Epistle of Paul to the Corinthians and the Epistles to Timothy, Titus and Philemon*, trans. by T. A. Smail (Grand Rapids: Eerdmans, 1964), p. 1.
40 Beza, *The Life of John Calvin*, p. 12.
41 Ganoczy, *The Young Calvin*, p. 91.

of Heidelberg from 1524 to 1529. He moved to the University of Basel where he taught Greek from 1529 to 1534. Grynaeus was a top-flight Greek philologist. He and Calvin became close friends, and they collaborated in studies regarding methods of exegesis. No doubt, Grynaeus significantly contributed to Calvin's study of and ability in the Greek language. Biblical Greek became one of Calvin's passions in life, and as Schaff concludes: 'He had passed through the school of the Renaissance; he had a rare knowledge of Greek; he thought in Greek, and could not help inserting rare Greek words into his letters to learned friends. He was an invaluable help to Luther in his translation of the Bible.'[42]

Calvin would wholeheartedly agree with Melanchthon's statement that 'the Scripture cannot be understood theologically unless it be first understood grammatically'. And, therefore, 'it must not be forgotten that Calvin was an intense student of the Bible in the original tongues.'[43] In truth, Calvin was an outstanding exegete.[44] Schaff rightly concludes that Calvin 'combined in a very rare degree all the essential qualifications of an exegete – grammatical knowledge, spiritual insight, acute perception, sound judgment, and practical tact.'[45] Indeed, the 'age of Calvin was one of translation and interpretation.'[46] For us to know Calvin the Reformer and Calvin the theologian, we must first know Calvin the exegete and linguist.[47] We now turn to view Calvin's ministry of preaching and the role played in it by the biblical languages.

---

42 P. Schaff, 'Calvin as a Commentator,' *The Presbyterian and Reformed Review* 3 (1892):463.

43 G. Johnson, 'Calvinism and Preaching,' *Evangelical Quarterly* 4 (1932):251.

44 T. Lane, 'The Quest for the Historical Calvin,' *Evangelical Quarterly* 55 (1983):113.

45 Schaff, 'Calvin as a Commentator,' p. 463.

46 Johnson, 'Calvinism and Interpretation,' p. 171.

47 Fuhrmann, 'Calvin, Expositor of Scripture,' p. 193.

Chapter Two

The Exegetical Preacher

As a preacher, 'Calvin's primary concern was to expound the scriptural revelation...'¹ He understood that for the preacher of the gospel 'exegesis will be his first line of duty; exposition his meat and drink.'² Calvin, in his preaching ministry, was true to these sound principles. Beeke properly summarizes Calvin's ministry of the word by saying, 'Calvin was a careful exegete, an able expositor, and a faithful applier of the Word.'³ The importance Calvin attached to his preaching was demonstrated on his deathbed. There at the end of his life, he reviewed his various ministries in his life, and in that review he talked more about his sermons than anything, even above that of his writing.⁴

During the decades of the 1540s and 1550s, Calvin was the

---

1 Lane, 'The Quest for the Historical Calvin,' p. 98.
2 J. H. Gerstner, 'Calvin's Two-Voice Theory of Preaching,' *Reformed Review* 13:2 (1959):17.
3 J. R. Beeke, 'Calvin as an Experiential Preacher,' *Evangelical Theological Society Paper* (2004):4.
4 *Opera* XXI:299. See, as well, Bouwsma, *John Calvin*, p. 29.

senior minister in Geneva. This position, as one would expect, entailed a considerable amount of preaching. Between 1541 and 1564, it has been estimated that Calvin preached no fewer than 4,000 sermons on the Bible. On the Old Testament alone he preached at least 2,000 sermons, and that figure only covers the years 1541 to 1556.[5] Calvin usually preached twice on Sundays, at dawn and at 3.00 p.m.; in the morning service he exposited a New Testament passage, and he tackled the Psalms in the afternoon. One or two mornings a week (6.00 a.m.), he would deliver a sermon on an Old Testament passage.[6]

Over 2,000 of Calvin's sermons have been preserved.[7] Unfortunately many others have been lost. Bouwsma comments on this point:

> Not all Calvin's sermons have yet been published; many, indeed, have disappeared. Early in the nineteenth century the pastor in charge of the Bibliothèque de Genève where they were stored sold most of the volumes of Calvin's manuscript sermons 'by weight,' that is, presumably as waste paper; and although some were eventually recovered, about a thousand were permanently lost.[8]

This painful and tragic story has been told in various places; for an account in English the reader ought to consult the work of T. H. L. Parker.[9]

Method of preaching

Calvin's method of preaching is well-documented: it was consecutive, expositional preaching through various books of the Bible. He would begin in verse 1, chapter 1 of a particular book and then preach through the book until the end. The next

---

5 T. H. L. Parker, *Calvin's Old Testament Commentaries* (Louisville: Westminster/John Knox Press, 1986), p. 10.
6 Johnson, 'Calvin and Preaching,' p. 249.
7 Hunter, 'Calvin as a Preacher,' p. 563.
8 Bouwsma, *John Calvin*, p. 244, n. 128.
9 T. H. L. Parker, *Supplementa Calviniana* (London: Tyndale Press, 1962).

sermon would begin a new book, and he would preach that book sequentially until finished. This is serial preaching at its best. Calvin's immediate movement to preach one book after another is what Gerstner calls 'chain preaching'.[10] He spent, for example, one year preaching through Job, a year and a half on Deuteronomy (200 sermons), and three years on Isaiah (350 sermons).

According to Beeke, 'The average length of texts covered in each of Calvin's sermons was four or five verses in the Old Testament and two or three verses in the New Testament. His sermons were fairly short for his day (perhaps due in part to his asthmatic condition), probably averaging thirty-five to forty minutes.'[11]

Calvin's primary purpose in the pulpit was to expound the Word of God. He believed this was the task of all preachers; and he said

> None must presume to obtrude himself and say, 'I am going to speak'. St. Peter wants us to have the assurance that when we go up into the pulpit we may show that God is sending us and that we are carrying the message which he has committed to us; so that 'he that speaks' (says he) 'let him speak as the Word of God' (1 Peter 4:11) – that is to say, that he shows by what he does that he is not intruding himself at his own will and that he is not mixing in anything of his dreams, but that he has and holds the pure truth of God.[12]

Fuhrmann gets at the heart of Calvin's preaching when he says that his sermons 'are properly homilies as in the ancient church: expositions of Bible passages at the light of grammar and history, and their application to the hearers' life situations.'[13] Calvin sought to understand Scripture itself, and to let the

---

10 Gerstner, 'Calvin's Two-Voice Theory of Preaching,' p. 25.
11 Beeke, 'Calvin as an Experiential Preacher,' p. 5.
12 *Opera* 54:286-87.
13 Fuhrmann, 'Calvin, the Expositor of Scripture,' p. 191.

Scriptures speak for themselves through the preacher.

In this regard, Calvin did not use contemporary issues of the day or the hot topics of the current socio-political issues of Europe in his preaching. It was not that Calvin was unaware of such issues swirling around him, but they are not the principal concern of the preacher. He said, 'I am not ignorant of what pleases or displeases the world, but nothing is of more concern to me than to follow the way the Master prescribes.'[14] On the other hand, Calvin did not shy away from using extrabiblical texts in order to explain a meaning of a Scriptural passage. Zachman comments that 'Calvin is convinced that the skilled interpreter of Scripture must be immersed in the literature of the Greek and Latin world and will often refer to such literature to help him elucidate the meaning of Scripture.'[15] This belief truly reflects Calvin's training in the ways and manners of the Renaissance.

Style of preaching

Calvin's style of preaching is also known to us. He would first scale the high pulpit in the church and then read his text of Scripture. When preaching from the Old Testament, he translated his text directly from the Hebrew Bible. Of the Hebrew texts available, Calvin likely used: the Hebrew Bible issued in Venice by Daniel Bomberg (d. 1549); the *Biblia Polyglotta Complutensia* (1514–1517), which included the Hebrew text, the LXX, the Vulgate, and a Hebrew vocabulary; and the Hebrew Bibles of Sebastian Münster (issued in Basel in 1536) and Robert Stephens (printed in Paris in 1539–1546).[16]

Reading from the New Testament prior to preaching, Calvin translated his text directly from the original Koine Greek language.[17] There is much disagreement among scholars

---

14 *Opera* 14:738.
15 R. C. Zachman, 'Gathering Meaning from the Context: Calvin's Exegetical Method,' *Journal of Religion* 82:1 (2002):11.
16 Johnson, 'Calvinism and Interpretation,' p. 171, n. 1.
17 See, especially, T. H. L. Parker, *Calvin's Preaching* (Louisville: Westminster/John Knox Press, 1992), pp. 172-78.

regarding which Greek text Calvin employed for his preaching, teaching, and writing. The conclusion by K. Erdos is perhaps the safest; he says, 'It is not possible to determine which Greek text was before Calvin.... But he certainly knew the editions of Erasmus, the editions of Stephanus and very probably the Complutensian edition.'[18] Parker argues that Calvin's use of Greek texts evolved from using Colinaeus as his basic text in his younger days to the Textus Receptus in his later days.[19] The reality is that Calvin was well-versed in many editions of the Greek text, and he felt at home in them and used many of them in his ministry.

Based on all available evidence, Calvin preached with no notes, but it was extemporary preaching directly from the original text. We have no manuscripts of Calvin's preaching extant from his own hand. Gerstner remarks, 'Calvin preached not only without a manuscript; not only without notes; but apparently without any outline whatever unless it was the order of the verses in the Bible itself.'[20] The only reason we have so many of his sermons is because a man named Denis Raguenier wrote them down in shorthand between the years 1549 and 1560 (the year of Raguenier's death). In this period of ten and a half years, Raguenier was able to take down about 2,000 of Calvin's sermons *ipsissima verba*, that is, word for word. There is no evidence that Calvin wanted these sermons published, but he knew that they were being recorded and printed. In a letter referring to a series of sermons on Psalm 8, Calvin said, 'They have been printed simply as they could be gathered from my mouth in the church. You there see our style and ordinary mode of teaching.'[21]

Calvin objected to read sermons. He was a 'pattern extempore preacher'.[22] He frequently intimated that the

---

18 Cited in T. H. L. Parker, *Calvin's New Testament Commentaries* (Louisville: Westminster/John Knox Press, 1993 ed.), p. 157.
19 Ibid., pp. 123-57.
20 Gerstner, 'Calvin's Two-Voice Theory of Preaching,' p. 22.
21 Bowman, 'Calvin as a Preacher,' p. 252.
22 Hunter, 'Calvin as a Preacher,' p. 563.

power of God could only pour forth most powerfully in extemporary preaching. In a letter to the Duke of Somerset, Calvin commented, 'I say this to your Highness because there is little of living preaching in your kingdom, sermons there being mostly read or recited.'[23]

Calvin's commitment to extemporary preaching does not mean that he had not done significant preparation prior to the sermon. He once commented:

> ... if I should climb up into the pulpit without having deigned to look at a book and frivolously imagine 'Ah well! When I get there God will give me enough to talk about,' and I do not condescend to read, or to think about what I ought to declare, and I come here without carefully pondering how I must apply the Holy Scripture to the edification of the people – well, then I should be a cock-sure charlatan and God would put me to confusion in my audaciousness.[24]

For Calvin, 'speaking without notes is one thing; speaking without preparation is quite another.'[25] The reality is that Calvin's lack of notes in preaching truly underscores his masterful preparation of the material being preached.

Calvin was probably asthmatical. Joseph Scaliger (1540–1609), a fine Huguenot scholar, often heard Calvin preach, and he called the reformer 'alone among the theologians'. He said that because Calvin had a weakness in the chest and was often short of breath he spoke slowly, deliberately, and with pauses.[26] Calvin also spoke slowly 'in order to give his hearers time to consider and digest what he had said.'[27] In addition, because he

---

23 Bowman, 'Calvin as a Preacher,' p. 252.
24 *Opera* 49:473-74. For translation, see Parker, *Calvin's Preaching*, p. 81.
25 Gerstner, 'Calvin's Two-Voice Theory of Preaching,' p. 24.
26 Scaliger was a top-flight scholar. He knew thirteen languages; among them were Greek, Hebrew, Aramaic, and Arabic. He ended his days as a research professor at the University of Leyden (1593–1609). He died in his students' arms. See G. W. Robinson, tr. *Autobiography of Joseph Scaliger* (Cambridge: Harvard University Press, 1927).
27 Hunter, 'Calvin as a Preacher,' p. 563.

spoke so deliberately, it was easy to write down all that he said. No doubt, Calvin's condition aided the amanuensis Raguenier in copying down all that Calvin said in his sermons.

Calvin 'abhorred and denounced long sermons and prayers. He himself is credited with having limited his discourses to half an hour's length.'[28] Part of this may have been due to his respiratory condition, that is, shortness of breath meant shortness of sermons. On the other hand, the brevity of the sermon is more likely due to Calvin's conviction regarding the purpose of a sermon. 'Directness, simplicity and brevity were the marks of a Calvinistic sermon.'[29] The preacher's task is to uncover the intended meaning of a passage in the original language, explain it to his congregation, and finally to apply it to his audience.[30] In regard to his sermon on Genesis 3:15, for example, he describes his movement from interpretation to application by saying, 'Since we have discovered the natural sense of this passage, let us now observe how it benefits us.'[31] Calvin disdained preaching that went above and beyond the sense and direct meaning of the text. He said, 'So when we enter the pulpit, it is not to bring there our dreams and fancies.'[32] Such simple and direct preaching as espoused by Calvin naturally lends itself to brevity.

---

28 Ibid., p. 563.

29 Gerstner, 'Calvin's Two-Voice Theory of Preaching,' p. 18.

30 Zachman puts it this way: 'In his sermons, Calvin guides the congregation in their reading of Scripture by showing how the genuine meaning of Scripture flows from the order of the context, and by drawing fruitful doctrine from that meaning. The bulk of his work as a preacher, unlike his work as a teacher, consists of applying that doctrine to the lives of the members of his congregation, and exhorting them to be transformed by the power of the doctrine they are hearing, which is none other than the power of Christ working by his Spirit.' See R. C. Zachman, ' "Do You Understand What You are Reading?" Calvin's Guidance for the Reading of Scripture,' *Scottish Journal of Theology* 54:1 (2001):12.

31 J. Calvin, *Sermons sur la Genèse, Chapitres 1.1-11.4* (Neukerchen-Vluyn: Neukirchener Verlag, 2000), p. 202. Cited in S. M. Manetsch, 'Problems with the Patriarchs: John Calvin's Interpretation of Difficult Passages in Genesis,' *Westminster Theological Journal* 67 (2005):10.

32 *Opera* 25:646.

Calvin eschewed what he called 'frivolous rhetoric,' that is, the rhetoric of the world.[33] Rather, he delighted in the simple and straightforward rhetoric of the Bible, and he attempted to imitate it in his preaching style and in his writing. In other words, he held to the clear brevity of the Word of God as paradigmatic for the simple eloquence of preaching from the pulpit.

Calvin loved preaching, and he continued preaching nearly to the end of his life. He died on May 27, 1564. We read that near the close of his life, when he was beset with infirmities and could not walk, he was carried in a chair to his well-loved and familiar pulpit. Colladon, who wrote a biography of Calvin in 1565, provides an account of these last days of preaching.

> ... his gout began to abate somewhat, and then he forced himself to go out sometimes to be entertained among his friends, but chiefly to lecture and even to preach, having himself carried to church in a chair ... he continued to do all he could of his public office, always dragging his poor body along, until the beginning of February 1564 ... on the Sunday, February 6, [he gave] his last sermon on the Harmony of the Three Gospels. Thereafter he never went up into the pulpit.[34]

Calvin's fortitude in preaching is reminiscent of many faithful men of the preaching ministry, such as John Newton.[35]

For our purposes, the fact that Calvin entered the pulpit carrying only his Hebrew Old Testament and his Greek New Testament underscores the man's phenomenal memory. But, more than that, it demonstrates his considerable ability

---

33 R. C. Gamble, '*Brevitas et Facilitas*: Toward an Understanding of Calvin's Hermeneutic,' *Westminster Theological Journal* 47 (1985):1-17.

34 *Opera* 21:96. Cited in Parker, *Calvin's Preaching*, p. 64.

35 Richard Cecil, a good friend of Newton's, counseled the preacher in his old age and feebleness. He suggested that Newton ought to consider his work done and so retire. Newton, in a clear and loud voice, answered him, 'I cannot stop. What, shall the old African blasphemer stop while he can speak?' See, B. H. Edwards, *Through Many Dangers: The Story of John Newton* (Darlington, England: Evangelical Press, 2001), p. 345.

to work with the original texts. Calvin may not have been an expert Hebraist and Greek scholar, along the lines of the contemporary Reuchlin or Scaliger, or the later Gesenius, but he had a thorough working knowledge of the Hebrew and Greek languages. He may not have been the top Hebraist or Greek master in Europe in his day, but he was highly capable and competent with those languages.

Chapter Three

King of Commentators

Calvin's commentaries

Calvin was a proficient author, and much of his writing was commentary work in which he expounded various books of the Bible. His commentaries were based upon his oral exposition of the biblical material to his congregation through his preaching and lecturing. At least three books of the Old Testament were being written at the same time in which they were being preached in the church at Geneva: the Psalms, the 'Mosaic', and Joshua. The preaching and teaching of Calvin served as a catalyst for his commentary work. He said he wrote (or perhaps privately dictated) his commentaries out of 'anxiety lest at some future time the transcript of my lectures might be published against my wishes or even without my knowledge.'[1]

In regard to the Old Testament, Calvin wrote commentaries that cover over sixty percent of the text. All four parts of the Hebrew canon received Calvin's written study comments. First, the Pentateuch was expounded with a full commentary

---

1 *Opera* 31:15-16; Parker, *Calvin's Old Testament Commentaries*, p. 30.

on Genesis, and then a harmony or 'mosaic' of Exodus through Deuteronomy. Joshua was the only written commentary in the historical literature, and Psalms was the only book Calvin tackled of the Wisdom literature. He commented on the prophets, both major and minor, in their entirety, except for Ezekiel, chapters 21–48. If one adds to this work the lecturing and preaching on the Old Testament that did not find its way into commentary form, then Calvin, in one way or another, expounded on approximately three-quarters of the books of the Old Testament.[2] The first to appear was a commentary on the Book of Isaiah (1551); it was followed by one on Genesis (1554), and then Psalms and Hosea (1557).

Virtually all of Calvin's Old Testament commentaries were written (or privately dictated) and first appeared in Latin. The only exception was the Book of Joshua that was composed and published in French. Why did Joshua appear first in French whereas the others were all first published in Latin? The answer is not known for certain, although several suggestions have been made. Parker offers the solution that Calvin wrote the commentary in French because it was a mere revision of what he had presented to his congregation in French.[3] Since the commentary was probably not finished at the time of his death, it may be that Calvin simply had no time to translate it into Latin.

Calvin's commentaries on the New Testament covered almost every book in the canon: the only ones missing were 2 John, 3 John, and the Book of Revelation. He also issued major revisions of the commentaries on the Pauline epistles much later in his life. Much of his New Testament commentary work preceded his Old Testament commentary writing. His commentary on Romans appeared in 1539–40, followed by 1 Corinthians (1546) and 2 Corinthians (1547 in French; 1548 in Latin); then came the Galatians grouping (1548), 1 and 2

---

2 Parker, *Calvin's Old Testament Commentaries*, p. 33.
3 Ibid., p. 33.

Timothy (1548), Hebrews (1549), and 1 and 2 Thessalonians (1550). All of those commentaries were published before his first Old Testament commentary that expounded the Book of Isaiah (1551).

Use of Hebrew in the commentaries
In his Old Testament commentaries, Calvin used the Hebrew language prodigiously and capably. For example, in his commentary work on Genesis 1–11, he made reference directly to the Hebrew text approximately forty times. I have studied each of these texts in depth for a recent Genesis commentary of my own.[4] In my opinion, there is little with which to quibble – most disagreements with Calvin in these references have nothing to do with linguistics but rather with issues of interpretation.

Much of Calvin's Hebrew work in Genesis 1–11 was lexical (i.e., word studies) rather than grammatical. For instance, he commented on Genesis 1:1 in regard to the word 'created':

> He (i.e., the author of Genesis) moreover teaches by the word 'created,' that what before did not exist was now made; for he has not used the term יָצַר, (y-ts-r) which signifies to frame or form, but בָּרָא, (b-r-‛) which signifies to create. Therefore his meaning is, that the world was made out of nothing.[5]

Although some commentators would disagree with Calvin's conclusion that בָּרָא (b-r-‛) inherently signifies *ex nihilo* creation, he was certainly correct in distinguishing between the sense of the two words יָצַר and בָּרָא (y-ts-r and b-r-‛). I state elsewhere:

> In ancient Hebrew a variety of words expressed the idea of 'making' or 'forming'. These words may have either God or mankind as the

---

4 J. Currid, *Genesis*, vol. 1, An EP Study Commentary (Darlington, England: Evangelical Press, 2003).
5 J. Calvin, *Commentaries on the First Book of Moses Called Genesis* (Grand Rapids: Baker, 1981), vol. 1, p. 70.

subject (e.g., 3:21; Exod. 38:1-3). The subject of the verb bara', however, is only and always God; the word is never used of an action of mankind (in the active Qal stem, as it appears here).⁶

Calvin's linguistic comments on Genesis 1–11 were not completely devoid of grammatical insights, however. One example appears in a brief comment he made on Genesis 6:4. Regarding the appearance of an unexpected Hebrew particle in the text, he said, 'In the context, the particle וגם, (w-g-m) which is interposed, is emphatical.'⁷ Calvin was correct here, for, indeed, that particle often has an emphatical force in biblical Hebrew.⁸ Another example emerges from Calvin's discussion of Genesis 9:5 when he commented on the first word of the verse. He said, 'I therefore think that Jerome, in rendering the particle אך, *for*, ('-k) has done better than they who read it as an adversative disjunctive; "*otherwise* your blood will I require;" yet literally it may best be thus translated, "And truly your blood."'⁹ His work here has demonstrated a proper understanding of the grammatical usage of this Hebrew adverb: it is often used in an adversative sense to demonstrate contrast, but, also, in an asseverative sense that emphasizes the expression of a truth.¹⁰

Calvin, in addition, employed etymological research in his commentaries. For instance, in his insights into the origin of the name Noah (Genesis 5:29), he rightly remarks:

> In the Hebrew language, the etymology of the verb נחם, (n-ch-m) does not correspond with the noun נוח, (n-w-ch) unless we call the letter מ, (m) superfluous; as sometimes, in composition, certain letters are redundant. נוח (n-w-ch) signifies to *give rest*,

---

6 Currid, *Genesis*, vol. 1, p. 59.
7 Calvin, *Commentaries on the First Book*, p. 245.
8 B. K. Waltke and M. O'Connor, *An Introduction to Biblical Hebrew Syntax* (Winona Lake, IN: Eisenbrauns, 1990), p. 663.
9 Calvin, *Commentaries on the First Book*, p. 294.
10 F. Brown, S. R. Driver, and C. A. Briggs, *A Hebrew and English Lexicon of the Old Testament* (Oxford: Clarendon Press, 1907), p. 36.

but נחם (n-ch-m) to *comfort*. The name Noah is derived from the former verb.[11]

In his use of etymology, Calvin was quite prudent. When dealing with the origin of the name of the people called Nephilim in Genesis 6:4, he stated,

> As to the Hebrew noun, נפלים, (n-p-l-y-m) its origin is known to be from the verb נפל, (n-p-l) which is *to fall*; but grammarians do not agree concerning its etymology.[12]

Calvin was hesitant to draw out too much from this etymology, and his discretion in these matters is good even by modern standards.[13]

The reformer was also quite familiar with numerous translations of the Hebrew text. In Genesis 1–11, he often made reference to and grappled with Jerome. And he did not hesitate to dispute Jerome's translation work. For example, Jerome (in the Latin) had translated Genesis 2:8 as 'But the Lord God had planted a paradise of pleasure from the beginning'. Calvin, in reference to Jerome's translation 'from the beginning' remarks that Jerome improperly translates this, from the beginning, is very obvious.'[14] The reformer rightly understood it to mean simply 'in Eden'. Calvin also made reference to the LXX, and at times agreed with its renderings and at other times he did not.[15]

Rabbinics

In his written commentaries, Calvin sometimes employed Jewish commentators when discussing a point of interpretation. He did not give a particular name or citation, but merely

---

11 Calvin, *Commentaries on the First Book*, p. 233.
12 Ibid., p. 244.
13 For valid criticisms of etymological studies, see J. Barr, *The Semantics of Biblical Language* (Oxford: Oxford University Press, 1961).
14 Calvin, *Commentaries on the First Book*, p. 113.
15 Ibid., p. 131.

referred to these authors as 'rabbis.'[16] Calvin used them primarily because of their lexicological expertise. As Puckett says, 'Calvin makes use of Jewish interpreters less frequently for grammatical than lexical help.'[17] In my opinion, Calvin was judicious in his usage of the Talmud and other post-biblical writings. He did not swallow their interpretations hook, line, and sinker. There was a certain underlying mistrust of the rabbinic exegesis and, therefore, Calvin was discriminating and restrained in integrating them into his biblical hermeneutic. For example, of the forty references to the Hebrew language in Genesis 1-11, Calvin rarely cites rabbinics and, then, only in a secondary fashion (see his comments on Genesis 2:8, 18; 6:3).

In his commentary work, Calvin sometimes outrightly rejects rabbinic interpretation. For instance, Calvin resolutely departed from the views of almost all Judaic scholarship in regard to the difficult reading of Psalm 22:16b. Whereas Judaism rendered the line 'like a lion my hands and my feet,' Calvin translated the Hebrew as 'they have pierced my hands and my feet.' The reformer truly and properly understood the lexical issue. He said,

> The original word, which we have translated *they have pierced*, is yrak, *caari*, which literally rendered is, *like a lion*. As all the Hebrew Bibles at this day, without exception, have this reading, I would have had great hesitation in departing from a reading which they all support, were it not that the scope of the discourse compels me to do so, and were there not strong grounds for conjecturing that this passage has been fraudulently corrupted by the Jews.[18]

---

16 This practice differed from Bucer who gave specific names as sources, such as Rashi, Kimchi, and Ibn Ezra. See, R. G. Hobbs, 'How Firm a Foundation: Martin Bucer's Historical Exegesis of the Psalms,' *Church History* 53:4 (1984):477-91.

17 Puckett, *John Calvin's Exegesis of the Old Testament*, p. 78, n. 60.

18 J. Calvin, *Commentary on the Book of Psalms* (Grand Rapids: Baker, 1979), p. 373.

Calvin's sane and sound practice of critically using rabbinics echoed the previous commentary work of Martin Bucer on the Psalms. Bucer 'would rely upon the exegetical and grammatical products of medieval Jewish scholars. None of their materials would be adopted uncritically, for their commentary had been deformed in varying degrees by their inability to penetrate to the heart of scripture – faith in Christ.'[19] Calvin himself acknowledged Bucer's influence on his commentary writing, when he said

> I expounded in our small school here the Book of Psalms about three years ago, and then decided not to publish about what I had familiarly deposited with my own household. In fact, even before I had undertaken the exposition at the request of my brethren, I spoke the truth in saying that I had refrained because that most faithful doctor of the Church of God, Martin Bucer, was preeminent in this work, with his outstanding learning, diligence, and fidelity; so there was, at any rate, not so much need for anything of mine.[20]

Indeed, Bucer's exegetical style of using the original Hebrew language, producing detailed Hebrew word studies, and a critical use of rabbinics was a pattern for reformed exegetes for many generations to come.

- Calvin did not trust the work of others who relied heavily on rabbinics. This distrust was one of the major points of disagreement and friction between Calvin and Michael Servetus. Servetus (1511–1553), a Spanish physician with theological interests, was internationally known for certain heretical views. Two charges continually leveled against Servetus were his anti-trinitarianism and that he was a 'judaizer'. Many believed that in his writings 'he exhibited an inappropriate tendency toward Judaism which he attempted

---

19 Hobbs, 'How Firm a Foundation,' p. 484.
20 *Opera* 31:13-14; cited in Parker, *Calvin's Old Testament Commentaries*, p. 30.

to pass on to his readers.'²¹ There was even speculation that Servetus was a *marrano*, that is, an insincere Jewish convert to Christianity.

Servetus did use rabbinics extensively and often mistakenly and uncritically. Much of his rabbinic work, not surprisingly, was used to support his modalism and anti-trinitarianism. For example, in regard to the Book of Isaiah, Servetus stripped it of having any messianic sense or prophecy in the same manner as the rabbis. Calvin responded that 'The perfidious scamp wrenches the passage so as to apply it to Cyrus.... Everyone will admit that I was right when I told him that no author had so boldly corrupted this signal prophecy.'²² Calvin demeaned Servetus by calling him 'this excellent rabbi' because he defended his theological positions with rabbinics.²³ Servetus answered Calvin by calling him a 'judaizer.'²⁴

The reality is that Servetus was culpable because he was guilty of extensive judaizing. Thus, he and Calvin were not only at odds in regard to the truths and doctrines of the church, but they clearly disagreed about the appropriate sources and their uses to arrive at good and sound theology.²⁵

Assessment of Calvin's use of Hebrew in the commentaries
Even by modern standards, Calvin's work in Hebrew in his Old Testament commentaries demonstrated great care and accuracy. His linguistic work did not, however, have great

---

21 J. Friedman, *Michael Servetus: A Case Study in Total Heresy* (Genève: Librairie Droz, 1978), p. 121.

22 *Opera* 8:496-7. See, as well, Friedman, *Michael Servetus*, p. 125.

23 Friedman, *The Most Ancient Testimony*, p. 174.

24 Even though Calvin was prudent in his use of rabbinics, the fact that he used Hebrew at all made him suspect to some people. The Lutheran author Hunnius, for instance, accused Calvin of being a 'judaizer.' See Friedman, *The Most Ancient Testimony*, p. 182.

25 To view some of the primary texts treating the confrontation between Servetus and the leadership in Geneva, see the recent study *A Reformation Reader: Primary Texts with Introductions*, ed. D. R. Janz (Minneapolis: Fortress Press, 1999), pp. 222-26.

depth and breadth to it. But certainly for his time he was an able and competent philologist. This by no means implies that Calvin was infallible in his use of biblical Hebrew or that we should not point out his mistakes in linguistic work.

For example, Calvin gave some countenance to an odd interpretation of Genesis 3:8a, which says, 'And they heard the voice of Yahweh God going forth in the garden in the wind of the day.' It appears that most scholars understand the expression 'in the wind of the day' in a temporal fashion. Some say it signifies sundown or late afternoon when breezes arise.[26] Others argue for the afternoon.[27] On the other hand, it may refer to the method by which God's voice is traveling through the garden. Calvin made the following comment on this expression, 'Others take the word as describing the southern part or region (i.e., of the garden); and certainly xwr, (r-w-ch) sometimes among the Hebrews signifies one or another region of the world.'[28] In reality, the use of this word in a spatial sense is not a meaning held in Scripture, except perhaps in a few quite obscure passages. Thus, Calvin's lexical work in this particular instance was a bit sloppy. A few other instances bear questionable interpretations based on linguistic study (e.g., comments on Genesis 3:15), but for the most part his work is solid.

Use of Greek in the commentaries
At the beginning of the sixteenth century the ancient Greek language was, for the most part, unknown. It was a mere curiosity even among the educated of Europe, almost a freakish field of study. Over the course of the century, however, great progress occurred in Europe in the study of Greek, so that by the end of it Greek had become an accepted, prominent field of study. D. Rebitté outlined three distinct periods of Greek study

---

26 E. A. Speiser, *Genesis*, vol. 1 (Garden City: Doubleday, 1964), p. 24.
27 U. Cassuto, *A Commentary on the Book of Genesis*, vol. 1 (Jerusalem: Magnes Press, 1961), p. 154.
28 Calvin, *Commentaries on the First Book*, p. 160.

in France during the sixteenth century.²⁹ The first, from 1500 to 1530, was characterized by a paucity of scholars doing Greek language work. In fact, Gillaume Budé almost stood alone as a proficient Greek scholar at this time. From 1530 to 1560 Greek study was in a pioneering period. It began with the founding of the trilingual royal institution in Paris, later to be known as the Collège de France. This period ended with the monumental Greek *Thesaurus* published by Henri Estienne in 1560. This period is the one in which Calvin performed all of his linguistic work: he was a second generation Greek scholar in the same way that he was a second generation reformer; his work came on the shoulders of others.³⁰ The final stage ran from 1560 to 1600. The study of Greek in France was now in full blossom, and in these years it received recognition as an appropriate and warranted area of academic study and research.

Calvin's learning of Greek began at the very beginning of Rebitté's second stage. Calvin, as mentioned earlier in our work, was a student at the Collège de France in its very early years. Based on that timing, he was greatly influenced by the work of Budé. In fact, throughout his commentary work, in particular, Calvin demonstrated a great literary dependence on Budé.³¹ Calvin may have also been influenced in his study of Greek in the early years at the Collège de France. In 1530, Francis I had appointed Pierre Danes to the chair of Greek at the college. And we know from a letter that Calvin wrote to Francis Daniel, dated June 27, 1531, that he intended to attend lectures by the venerable Danes.³² How many lectures he may have attended and the extent of his contact with Danes is a matter of speculation.

---

29 D. Rebitté, *Gillaume Budé restaurateur des études grecques en France* (Paris: essai historique, 1846).

30 Breen, *John Calvin: A Study in French Humanism*, p. 131.

31 See, especially, J. Bohatec, *Budé und Calvin* (Wien: Verlag Hermann Bohlaus Nachf, 1950).

32 Battles, *Interpreting John Calvin*, p. 61.

Calvin's Greek study progressed rapidly during the early part of the decade of the 1530s. Indeed, in 1535, Calvin was already accepted by Olivetan as one competent enough in the Greek language to assist in the translation of the New Testament.[33] Over the next few years, Calvin used his Greek prodigiously in order to produce his first commentary, namely, on the Book of Romans. He wrote the dedication to the commentary on October 18, 1539, and it was published in the early part of the following year. The commentary was perhaps based on a series of lectures he had been giving, beginning in 1536, on the Pauline corpus. A printer from Basel named Oporinus wrote Calvin in 1537, and he said, 'I hear you are lecturing with great applause and usefulness on St. Paul's Epistles.'[34] No doubt, much Greek work was done for these lectures, and then found its way into the written commentaries.

Much of his New Testament commentary work occurred in the 1540s, and in that work we can see maturity, confidence, and great care in Calvin's use of the Greek language. For his day, Calvin was an excellent Greek scholar. In truth, he had greater ease with and could work better with Greek than he could with Hebrew. His Hebrew was good but his Greek was outstanding.

A good example of his prowess for his time was his great care in establishing what he thinks is the most reliable Greek text. He performed work in textual criticism: he was well aware of variants and alternate Greek readings. He worked meticulously and diligently to establish the best text. Parker comments, 'But however he came by his textual material it is clear that Calvin's first task in preparing his translation was to establish a text with which he could be satisfied. It is also clear that he was not concerned only with the more important places but paid close attention to every sentence.'[35]

A number of Greek texts were available to Calvin. In his

---

33 Parker, *Calvin's New Testament Commentaries*, p. 14.
34 *Opera* 10:91.

earliest commentary work he appears to have relied most heavily upon the Greek text of Colinaeus of 1534. Calvin did not accept *en toto* this text, however. Other texts and variants are found even in these early commentaries. After 1548, in his later commentary work, Calvin seemed to have depended mostly on the Greek textual work of Erasmus. The first edition of Erasmus' text appeared in 1516 and until around the time of Calvin's death approximately thirty editions of the text were published and in print. Parker suggests that Calvin probably used the 4th edition (1527) as his principal text in the later commentaries.[36] Again, he did not feel obliged to stick to that text only; there were comments in the works that indicate he also employed the Colinaeus text and a Stephanus text at this time.

Calvin did not shy away from performing tasks of textual criticism. He corrected many readings of the available texts without hesitation. For example, although much of his labor in the Greek text of the Pauline epistles was based on the Colinaeus edition, he corrected many of the readings of that text. He did this both at the time of their initial publication and in the revisions that appeared in the mid-1550s. His use of textual criticism, as would be expected, was rudimentary because of his limited resources and the lack of commentators before him who did such work.

Once Calvin had established the best text, he almost always translated directly from that original Greek text. He knew and used the Vulgate, but he did not trust it in the way that he trusted the original. Only rarely did he depart from the Greek text. He would translate it literally into Latin, and then make comments on the text.

---

35 Parker, *Calvin's New Testament Commentaries*, p. 151.
36 Parker, *Calvin's New Testament Commentaries*, p. 153.

Conclusion

In summary, Calvin's commentary work was securely anchored in his linguistic study in the original biblical languages of Hebrew and Greek. And that is a primary reason that his work was fresh and engaging for the day in which he wrote, and it is also one reason that his labors continue to influence biblical scholarship of our own day. Calvin was competent in the Hebrew language, but, honestly, he was better in Greek. Perhaps that reflects his day and age in which the Greek language seems to have gained easier acceptance within the academic community at an earlier date. Hebrew, obviously, was tied to Judaism, and an air of anti-Semitism in the sixteenth century perhaps denied Hebrew study its proper place in academia.

Chapter Four

This Most Faithful Interpreter

The Teacher

In the *Institutes of the Christian Religion* (first published in 1536), John Calvin explained that in his view both pastors and teachers 'have an ordinary office in the Church.'[1] Luther would have agreed with this statement, yet Calvin 'was more clear on the difference between a preacher and a teacher than Luther had been.'[2] Calvin stated:

> ... there is this difference, that teachers preside not over discipline, or the administration of the sacraments, or admonitions, or exhortations, but the interpretation of Scripture only, in order that pure and sound doctrine may be maintained among believers. But all these are embraced in the pastoral office.[3]

To Calvin, a pastor is to be primarily concerned with a local charge, but the teacher's function is to promote and maintain

---

[1] *Institutes* Book IV, Ch. 3, Section 4.
[2] E. Harris Harbison, *The Christian Scholar in the Age of the Reformation* (New York: Scribner's, 1956), p. 155.
[3] *Institutes* Book IV, Ch. 3, Section 4.

sound instruction and doctrine in the Church at large.[4]

When Calvin first settled in Geneva in the late 1530s he called himself 'Lecturer in Holy Scripture in the Church of Geneva.' He was a teacher at first, but he was soon called to preach as well. During his whole life he considered himself to be both a teacher and a preacher of the Bible, and he truly understood these two callings as feeding off one another.

When Calvin lectured in Geneva, beginning in the 1540s and later at the Academy (1559), his methodology of teaching was one of consistency. According to Budé, who heard Calvin lecture often, the Reformer would begin his lecture with prayer. Budé commented, 'For as at the beginning of the Lectures he ever used the same form of prayer...'[5] We do not know the content of these opening prayers as they were not included in the commentaries, but we do know from Budé's statement that they were general and similar in nature to one another.

Calvin would then read a text in Hebrew or Greek, and offer a very literal translation of it into Latin. After that, he would provide a smoother Latin translation, followed by his commentary.[6] Jean Crispin, a publisher of Calvin's day, attended some of the reformer's lectures. He commented on Calvin's lecture style as follows: '... but he kept on lecturing continuously for a full hour and did not write down one single word in his book to help his memory.'[7] The book in question was the Hebrew Old Testament and, thus, Calvin was sight-reading the Hebrew text without any linguistic aids. Then, also without notes, he made comment on the text that had been read.

Colladon also remarked on Calvin's teaching style; he said:

> When lecturing, he always had only the bare text of Scripture; and yet, see how well he ordered what he said! Even when (some

---

[4] J. T. McNeill, *The History and Character of Calvinism* (New York: Oxford University Press, 1954), p. 218.

[5] *Preface to Calvin's Commentaries on the Twelve Minor Prophets*, vol. 1 (Grand Rapids: Baker, 1981), p. xxviii.

[6] Puckett, *John Calvin's Exegesis*, p. 59.

[7] Quoted in Parker, *Calvin's Old Testament Commentaries*, p. 20.

years before his death) he was lecturing on Daniel, although at some places he had to narrate historical facts at length, as we see from the lectures, he never had any paper before him as an aide-mémoire. And it was not as if he had adequate time to prepare; for, whatever he may have wished, he simply had not the opportunity. To say the truth, he usually had less than an hour to prepare.[8]

Calvin would end his lectures in prayer. Budé commented, 'For as at the beginning of the Lectures he ever used the same form of prayer, which we intend also to add, that his manner of teaching may be fully known to you; so he was wont ever to finish every Lecture by a new prayer formed at the time, as given him by the Spirit of God, and accommodated to the subject of the Lecture.'[9] The point of Budé's statement was to contrast the opening prayer of a lecture and its closing prayer: the first was formal and general; the last was adapted to the subject of the lecture and delivered extemporaneously and by the power of the Holy Spirit.

One example of a closing prayer for a lecture appears in his commentary on Hosea 1:1-2. That passage deals with the obstinate Israelites who have refused to obey God and his word. After commenting on the verses, Calvin concludes with this prayer:

> Grant, Almighty God, that as thou hast once adopted us, and continuest to confirm this thy favour by calling us unceasingly to thyself, and dost not only severely chastise us, but also gently and paternally invite us to thyself, and exhort us at the same time to repentance, – O grant that we may not be so hardened as to resist thy goodness, nor abuse this thine incredible forbearance, but submit ourselves in obedience to thee; that whenever thou mayest severely chastise us, we may bear thy corrections with genuine submission of faith, and not continue untameable and

---

8 *Opera* 21:108-9. See, Parker, *Calvin's Old Testament Commentaries*, p. 21, n. 25.
9 *Preface to Calvin's Commentaries on the Twelve Minor Prophets*, p. xxviii.

obstinate to the last, but return to thee, the only fountain of life and salvation, that as thou hast once begun in us a good work, so thou mayest perfect it to the day of our Lord. Amen.[10]

The deliverance of the lectures was not characterized by elegance of style or by flowery oration, which apparently was a common means of teaching in that day. According to Budé, Calvin 'preferred to advance the edification and benefit of his hearers by eliciting the true sense and making it plain, rather than by vain pomp of words to delight their ears, or to regard ostentation and his own glory.'[11] Budé portrays Calvin's lecture style as more scholastic than oratorical. The point which Budé was making is that Calvin taught in a clear, simple, and direct way in the Latin language. Precisely what Budé meant by 'scholastic' is hard to know for certain. Does it refer to medieval scholars and their manner of teaching? Does it signify some type of scholarly teaching that would be opposed to popular speaking? It seems most likely, although this may be speculation, that Budé was using this term to define Calvin's teaching style as formal, logical, methodical, and practical. It was straight-forward and in no way intended to tickle the ears of his audience.

In his teaching, Calvin was well known for his clarity and his ability to get at the heart of a text. In the preface to the commentary on the Book of Daniel, the publisher commented on Calvin's pedagogy: 'I present to thee the Lectures of the most illustrious John Calvin, in which he has interpreted the prophecies of Daniel, with his usual diligence and clearness, and with that singular fidelity which shines throughout all his Expositions of Sacred Scripture.'[12] And, again, the preface includes the statement: 'It is exceedingly agreeable to Hebrew scholars to have that very fountain placed before their eyes

---

10 *The Commentaries of John Calvin on the Prophet Hosea* (Grand Rapids: Baker, 1981), pp. 46-47.
11 *Preface to Calvin's Commentaries on the Twelve Minor Prophets*, p. xxvii.

from which this most faithful Interpreter drew the genuine sense of the Prophet.'[13]

As is clear *ad nauseum*, Calvin's students were expected to know Hebrew, Greek and Latin. Calvin taught in Latin on the original texts of the Bible written in Hebrew and Greek. He did extensive word studies, literary work, and he dealt with all manner of biblical Hebrew syntax. Quite aware of Hebrew idiom in the original, he often compared it with idiomatic expressions from both Greek and Latin. He frequently based his interpretation of biblical passages solely on points of Hebrew and Greek grammars. A student without the working knowledge of these three languages would have been academically lost.

It seems likely that Calvin lectured three days a week in alternate weeks. And these lectures occurred on three consecutive days in the week. According to Parker, each lecture normally lasted for a full hour – Calvin sometimes mentions during his lectures that his allotted hour was just about over.[14] Obviously, with all of his duties his lectures were sometimes disrupted and, thus, either shortened or cancelled. For example, one time he had to end a lecture early because of some urgent intrusion: he said, 'I wish I could proceed further, but I have some business to which I was called before the lecture.'[15]

Often the lectures served as the source for Calvin's written commentaries: such is the stated case for his commentary on the Book of Daniel, for instance. But this is not true for all the commentaries. Lectures sometimes acted as a mere stimulus for the commentary, but not much more than that. For example, his lectures on the Book of Psalms were partially used for his later written commentary, but much more work was needed and done for the final written exposition.

---

12 *Preface to Calvin's Commentaries on the Prophet Daniel* (Grand Rapids: Baker, 1981), p. lxii.
13 Ibid., p. lxii.
14 Parker, *Calvin's Old Testament Commentaries*, p. 21.
15 *Opera* 37:499.

Chapter Five

The Academy

The vision
In 1536, by the urging of Farel, the leadership of Geneva (the Small Council and the Council of Two Hundred) agreed to adopt the Reformation.[1] Farel further entreated the leadership to seek approval from the assembly of all the citizens of Geneva. 'By unanimous decision, the community voted to live by the Word of God and to establish a school for their children.'[2] The resolution regarding the founding of a school in Geneva reads as follows:

> The General Council, 21 May 1536
> At this session was also proposed the provision concerning the schools, upon which it was resolved by a unanimous vote that the city endeavor to have a learned man to effect this and that he

---

1 Guillaume Farel (1489–1565) was a French Protestant reformer who was a fearless evangelist for the cause of the Reformation. He enlisted Calvin to assist in the organization of Geneva as a new Protestant city. Farel was a close confidant and friend of Calvin throughout his life.
2 R. M. Kingdon, ed. *Transition and Revolution: Problems and Issues of European Renaissance and Reformation History* (Minneapolis: Burgess Pub. Co., 1974), p. 96.

be paid enough so that he may nourish himself and instruct the poor without asking any fees of them, and also, that everyone be required to send his children to the school and have them learn. And, all the students and teachers are required to reside in the great school where the rector and his assistant instructors, *bacheliecs*, will be.[3]

Farel founded a school in Geneva in 1536 and 'it progressed for some years but by the year 1550 it had retrogressed to such an extent that many parents had to send their children to other cities for the necessary instruction.'[4]

Calvin was expelled from Geneva in May of 1538. Bucer invited him to Strassburg where Calvin pastored a congregation of French refugees for three years. Calvin, at the urging of Bucer, returned to Geneva in September, 1541. His first concern was to set up the church in Geneva according to the principle that 'the church cannot stand firm unless a government is constituted as prescribed to us by the Word of God and observed in the early church.'[5] Calvin insisted that the city's leadership agree to a formal, written declaration of the organization of the Genevan church. They agreed, and under the supervision of Calvin, *The Ecclesiastical Ordinances of 1541* came into being.

The ordinances describe and explain the four orders of offices for the government of the Genevan church: pastors, doctors/teachers, elders, and deacons. In regard to the second order, namely doctors/teachers, the ordinances call for the establishment of a *collège*. The text reads:

> The proper office of the doctors is to instruct the faithful in sound doctrine so that the purity of the Gospel is not corrupted either by ignorance or by erroneous belief.... Thus, to use a more

---

3 Ibid., p. 97.
4 J. Chr. Coetzee, 'Calvin and the School,' in *John Calvin: Contemporary Prophet*, ed. J. T. Hoogstra (Grand Rapids: Baker, 1959), p. 205.
5 *Opera* 11:281; this appears in a letter to Farel dated September 16, 1541.

intelligible word, we shall call it the order of the schools. The degree nearest to the ministry and most closely associated with the government of the Church is the lectureship in theology which rightly includes both the Old and New Testament. However, since it is possible to profit from such lessons only if first instructed in languages and the humanities, and since also there is need to raise up the seed for the future so that the Church is not left a desert to our children, a *collège* must be established in order to instruct them and to prepare them for the ministry as well as for the civil government.[6]

Two important points to be gleaned from Calvin's early vision reflected in *The Ecclesiastical Ordinances of 1541* need to be noted because they are foundational to his lifelong educational program. First, Calvin at this early time desired to have a *collège* that has a two-fold purpose of instruction: one is to prepare children to become good, godly citizens no matter their calling, whether it be in ministry or in civil government. The other is specifically to train ministers for gospel preaching. Second, the foundation of all education at the *collège* is 'in languages and the humanities.' Calvin's lifelong commitment to language instruction set him apart from most educators of his day. Walker puts it this way: Calvin wanted a school in Geneva 'effective in its methods, especially in instilling a fundamental basis of philological learning, and having its crown instruction in theology, by which pastors could be trained for the service of the Church.'[7]

Beginnings of the Academy (1558)[8]
It was not until 1558 that there occurred any significant progress in regard to Calvin's educational vision. But 'in January 1558,

---

6 Kingdon, *Transition and Revolution*, p. 100.
7 W. Walker, *John Calvin: The Organiser of Reformed Protestantism, 1509-1564* (New York: Schocken Books, 1969), p. 360.
8 For a brief overview, see A. L. Weidman, *The Embodiment of Calvin's Humanism in the Establishment of the Academy of Geneva in 1559* (Portland, OR: Tren, 1998).

the Little Council, at Calvin's instigation, ordered the selection of a site for a "College".[9] Calvin immediately began raising money for buildings to be erected on the site. Construction began in April 1558, but the buildings were not completed until 1562. Many of these structures survive to the present day.

At that time Calvin also began a search to enlist competent faculty. He was able to get approval from the leadership in Geneva to hire such persons. In a letter (1558) to Immanuel Tremellius Calvin said, 'I have at last obtained of the senate that professors of three languages should be appointed' to the Academy.[10] Calvin thus secured three chairs for the school: in Latin, Greek, and Hebrew. Initially, Calvin had a difficult time finding professors for the Academy faculty. Part of the hardship stemmed from a severe lack of funds. The reality is that Calvin was in no position to offer adequate compensation to the professors that he invited. Geneva was not a wealthy city and, thus, Calvin's efforts were greatly hindered in these early days.

Calvin's problem was partially solved by an unexpected theological controversy in the city of Lausanne. There a school had been founded in 1537 based on some lectures given by Viret. Since that time the school had flourished as a place of training for French-speaking Protestants. Two of the leaders at Lausanne, Viret and Beza, 'fully sympathised with Calvin's ecclesiastical discipline; and, in March 1558, they tried to introduce there his independent right of excommunication.'[11] The authorities of the civil government wanted nothing to do with it and, therefore, some of the ministers and faculty at Lausanne were in untenable positions. Many of them fled the city, and they came to Geneva.

---

9 Walker, *John Calvin*, p. 361; see, as well, A. Roget, *Histoire du people de Geneve depuis la reforme jusqu'à l'esralade*, 7 vols. (Geneva, 1870–83); see vol. 5, p. 227.

10 J. Bonet, *Letters of John Calvin*, vol. 3 (New York: Burt Franklin reprints, 1973), pp. 464-65.

11 Walker, *John Calvin*, p. 362.

This exodus from Lausanne was a boon to Calvin: he now had many of his teachers for the Academy. Beza immediately accepted the Greek chair; he would, however, never hold the chair because he was soon appointed Rector of the Academy. He was replaced by François Bérauld as Professor of Greek. Jean Tagaut, another Lausanne refugee, agreed to the Latin chair. Calvin's attempts to fill the Hebrew chair met with little success at first.

> Both Jean Mercier of the trilingual college in Paris and Immanuel Tremellius, who was at that time lecturing in Heidelberg, politely refused his invitation. But with his third choice he was lucky. Anthony Chevallier, recently expelled from the Bernese Academy in Lausanne together with several other scholars, gladly accepted the post. According to the regulations he was to give eight hours of Hebrew instruction per week, five of which were to be devoted to grammar and three to the exposition of 'some books of the Old Testament with the rabbinic commentaries.'[12]

Chevallier was a master Hebraist who once was the tutor in French of Princess Elizabeth, who became Queen of England. Chevallier left the Academy in 1567 to take a chair in Hebrew at Cambridge University. He died in 1572.

'In March and May 1559, the registers of the small council recorded the presentation and acceptance of Antoine Le Chevallier as professor of Hebrew, Francois Bérauld as professor of Greek, and Jean Tagaut as professor of philosophy.'[13] Borgeaud reports that they were to earn 280 florins per year, an amount that paid them between the regents and the ministers on the salary scale of Geneva.[14]

---

12 Lloyd Jones, *The Discovery of Hebrew*, pp. 77-78.
13 K. Maag, *Seminary or University? The Genevan Academy and Reformed Higher Education, 1560-1620* (Aldershot Hants, England: Scolar Press, 1995), p. 14.
14 C. Borgeaud, *Histoire de l'université de Genève: L'Académie de Calvin 1559-1798* (Geneva, 1900), p. 41.

Establishment of the Academy (1559)

The next step in the creation of the Academy was the adoption of a constitution that set down the regulations for the operation of the institution. It was called the *Leges Academiae Genevensis*, and it was approved by the Little Council on May 22, 1559.[15] There is some debate regarding the author of this work, although it cannot be denied that Calvin's imprint is all over the document. The constitution is perhaps largely based on the educational pioneering work of J. Sturm in Strassburg; Calvin, of course, would have been quite familiar with that work since he resided in Strassburg between 1538 and 1541.

As an aside, the establishment of the school in Geneva occurred in most perilous times. According to Beza, Henry III of France was plotting to 'completely overthrow Geneva' in 1559. Calvin went to great measures to insure the defeat of those designs. Beza comments:

> But Geneva, by the singular providence of God, as if the Lord were again and again causing the purest light to arise out of the thickest darkness, experienced at that time an almost incredible confidence. In the same year, and almost at the very moment when these powerful princes were conspiring her destruction, it gave orders, on the suggestion of Calvin, for the erection of a magnificent building for a school, provided with eight teachers of youth and public professors of Hebrew, Greek, Philosophy and Theology.[16]

On June 5, 1559 a ceremony of dedication took place in a full assembly of people in the main church of St. Pierre. A cross-section of people from Geneva were in attendance: ministers, magistrates, faculty, students, and common folk of the town. Calvin opened the time with prayer. He was followed by Michel Roset who read the laws regarding the maintenance of the school and its confession of faith. Beza, the first rector of the school, gave the opening convocation address. His salient

---

15 *Opera* 21:716.
16 Beza, *The Life of John Calvin*, p. 51.

point was that the Academy was not merely a place to get a good education but it 'was to provide goal-oriented training, with an especial, although not exclusive, focus on theology and on the mission which the students were called to fulfil, both as ministers and as laymen in the Calvinist world.'[17]

Structure of the Academy and its curriculum

The Genevan Academy had two departments: the *schola private* (the lower department) and the *schola publica* (the upper level). The former was for children beginning school at six years of age. There were seven levels of education; the seventh class was the most rudimentary and the first class was the highest order in the school. The content of the various levels are well-known and we do not need to repeat them here.[18] When one reads them, however, one is immediately struck by the amount and centrality of the linguistic work. Bilingual instruction commenced in level seven, that is, the opening grade: students began to learn both French and Latin at this early age. By the fourth class they were introduced to the Greek language. In the upper three class levels the students were preparing almost all of their work in the original languages of Latin and Greek: they read, for example, Homer, Virgil, Cicero from their original tongues. They also translated directly from the New Testament; in level two they were reading the Gospel of Luke and in level one they were translating the Epistles.

The *schola private* served as a feeder to the *schola publica*; the latter had its primary purpose to train future ministers of the gospel. These were students who were preparing to preach the Word of God. And since 'the exposition of the Bible was central to the sermon, Calvin ensured that the biblical languages were given primary place in the curriculum.'[19]

---

17 Maag, *Seminary or University?*, p. 16.
18 *Opera Selecta* 2:368-70.
19 Lloyd Jones, *The Discovery of Hebrew*, p. 77. Calvin's interest in Hebrew, in particular, was reflected in the library holdings of the Academy. Lloyd Jones

Walker concludes that Calvin's purpose was to 'make Geneva the theological seminary of Reformed Protestantism.'[20] To Calvin, the Academy was to be an institution of great learning. And he believed that *erudition* required mastery of three languages: Hebrew, Greek, and Latin.

The curriculum of the *schola publica* was constituted and organized in *The Order of the Geneva Schools*.[21] It is appropriate to quote the entire section at this point, although it is lengthy:

> The three public Lecturers that is, in Hebrew, Greek and in Arts, shall be elected and confirmed as the others.
>
> On Monday, Tuesday and Thursday each of them shall lecture for two hours, one hour in the morning and one hour after dinner. On Wednesday and Friday each one shall lecture for one hour, that is after dinner. On Saturday they shall have no lessons. Sunday shall be employed hearing sermons.
>
> Friday they shall, if possible, be present at the Congregation and at the Colloquy of the Ministers.
>
> The Professor of Hebrew shall explain in the morning, immediately after the sermon, some book of the Old Testament with the Hebrew commentaries. After dinner he shall lecture on Hebrew grammar, in the winter from midday to one o'clock, and in the summer from one o'clock to two.
>
> The Professor of Greek shall, in the morning immediately after the Hebrew lecture, explain some book of Moral Philosophy. The book shall be of Aristotle or Plato or Plutarch or some Christian philosopher. After dinner he shall lecture (in winter from one to two o'clock, in the summer from three to four) on a Greek poet or some orator or historian, at one time taking one type and another time another, but choosing the purest.
>
> The Professor of Arts shall come in the morning after the Professor of Greek and shall expound some book of physical

---

remarks, 'It is noteworthy that there were far more books on the Old Testament than on the New; a sure indication that from Calvin's time onwards the Jewish Bible was given pride of place in Geneva. The study of it was rooted in the original language...' (p. 78).

20 Walker, *John Calvin*, p. 366.

21 *Opera Selecta* 2:368-70.

science for half an hour. After dinner (in winter from three to four o'clock and in summer from four to five) he shall expound learnedly the *Rhetoric* of Aristotle, the most famous *Speeches* of Cicero or the books of *De Oratore*.

The two Professors of Theology shall expound the books of Holy Scripture Monday, Tuesday and Wednesday from two o'clock after dinner to three, each one in his week.[22]

Calvin's enthusiasm for biblical studies at the core of the curriculum of the *schola publica*, in addition to his trilingual training as a student in Paris, secured a prominent place for Hebrew, Greek, and Latin in the Genevan course of study. 'Future Calvinist ministers learned Hebrew by studying the Old Testament, perfected their Greek and Latin by further analysis of classical authors, went more deeply into history, and learned physics from Aristotle.'[23] Calvin wanted for the Academy a deep integration of the Reformed faith with a strong classical curriculum that heavily emphasized study of original languages. Battles comments:

> Compare also Calvin's premature attempts to learn the Greek language with the orderly introduction of that tongue to pupils at age eleven or twelve. Calvin himself probably did not master Greek until he was twenty-five years of age. He realized how crucial a knowledge of Greek was for the understanding of the New Testament. And his fluency in Hebrew probably came to him still later than that in Greek; the typical Geneva student, on the other hand, was to undertake the study of Hebrew, if he moved without delay from the *schola privata* to the *schola publica*, in his middle teens.[24]

Calvin was disturbed by theologians who denounced language study 'with furious zeal' and 'who level as many

---

[22] W. Stanford Reid, 'Calvin and the Founding of the Academy of Geneva,' *Westminster Theological Journal* 18 (1955-56):31-2.
[23] Bouwsma, *John Calvin*, pp. 14-15.
[24] F. L. Battles, *Interpreting John Calvin* (Grand Rapids: Baker, 1996), p. 63.

reproaches as they can' against the pursuit of acquiring skill in the original languages.[25] He believed that ignorance of biblical languages resulted in mistakes in matters 'easy and obvious to every one' and those without skills are led 'most shamefully astray.'[26] He concurred fully with the old rabbinic adage that studying the Bible without Hebrew is like kissing one's bride through the veil. In the Academy curriculum, Calvin 'emphasised even more than the earlier educational reformers the value of thorough preparatory linguistic studies.'[27]

Purpose of the *schola publica*
The creation of the Academy was perhaps Calvin's crowning achievement. However, it needs to be noted that Calvin's purpose in establishing this enterprise was not merely to produce scholars. In reality, 'one of its chief titles to renown has always been, up to very recent times, that of having formed a body of pastors provided with a high degree of intellectual culture.'[28] His aim in the *schola publica* was to raise up and train pastor-scholars. These were men who could work well with the original languages of Hebrew and Greek, who could perform proper exegesis of a text, and who understood theology and philosophy; yet, they could take all that intellectual work and translate it to the masses. These were pastor-scholars who did not stay in the ivory tower, but they sought to find the truth and then apply it to the people. The purpose of the academic work was to affect the church and the world with the truth and power of the Word of God. Calvin himself was such a pastor-scholar. A true comparison has been made that says:

---

25 J. Calvin, *Commentary on the Epistles of Paul the Apostle to the Corinthians*, vol. 1 (Grand Rapids: Baker, 1981), p. 437.
26 J. Calvin, *Institutes of the Christian Religion* (Grand Rapids: Eerdmans, 1962), Book IV, Chapter XIX, Section 36.
27 Walker, *John Calvin*, p. 365.
28 F. Wendel, *Calvin: The Origins and Development of His Religious Thought* (New York: Harper & Row, 1963), p. 105.

Erasmus addressed his scholarly works to men of learning, hoping (as he said in his Paraclesis) that the results would trickle down to the people by translation. Luther was very diffident about addressing scholars and did his finest work in translating the Bible into the vernacular in order to reach everyone, even the most humble, in his native land. Calvin sensed the importance of both objectives with his usual acumen and sense of balance.[29]

The legacy of the Geneva Academy
By almost any standards, the founding of the Academy was a success. By the time of Calvin's death (1564), a mere five years after the establishment of the school, 1,200 students were attending the *schola private* and 300 were enrolled in the *schola publica*.[30] In the ensuing years, the Academy became even more influential. Gamble remarks that 'the most important change to occur in the Academy of Geneva was its development under Beza's leadership into the most famous center of Protestant learning in Europe.'[31]

Most of the students in the *schola private* were from Geneva, while a majority of those in the *schola publica* were from foreign countries. Walker comments:

> Within three years of its opening, it numbered among its scholars such names as those of Kaspar Olevianus, to be one of the two authors of the Heidelberg Catechism, of Philippe de Marnix de Saint-Aldegonde, of Netherlandish memory; of Florent Chrestien, tutor of Henry IV of France; of Thomas Bodley, the founder of the library known by his name at the English Oxford; of Francis

---

29 E. Harris Harbison, *The Christian Scholar in the Age of the Reformation* (New York: Scribner's, 1956), p. 159.

30 Borgeaud, *Histoire de l'Université de Genève*, pp. 160-65. The important studies regarding numbers of students attending the school over the centuries are: S. Stelling-Michaud, ed. *Le Livre du Recteur de l'Académie de Genève (1559-1878)*, 6 vols. (Geneva: Droz, 1959–1981); and M. Heyd, *Between Orthodoxy and the Enlightenment* (The Hague: Martinus NIJHOFF Pub., 1982), pp. 245-88.

31 R. C. Gamble, 'Switzerland: Triumph and Decline,' in *John Calvin: His Influence in the Western World*, ed. W. Stanford Reid (Grand Rapids: Zondervan, 1982), p. 66.

Junius, later to be the ornament of the University of Leyden. France, England, Scotland, the Netherlands, Germany, Italy, and Switzerland had their representatives; but France most of all.[32]

The Academy at Geneva had a great impact upon university education throughout Europe. For example, it was the model for the University of Leiden in Holland. 'Leiden was founded in 1575 and was quickly followed by Franeker, Groningen, Utrecht and Harderwijk. All were Calvinistic centers and began to attract foreign students in the fashion of Geneva, especially as zeal declined in Geneva and the center of Calvinism shifted northward. Holland became the major center for the exporting of Calvinism.'[33]

In Britain, higher level education was greatly affected by the Genevan system. The Academy's influence on the establishment of the University of Edinburgh is obvious. 'Unlike the medieval autonomy of the faculty and nations of the medieval university, Edinburgh was placed under the civil administration and the ministers of the city. This meant much more control of the curriculum and faculty. The university was intended to serve the church.'[34] The Academy was also the pattern for Emmanuel College at Cambridge.

In regard to language study, Geneva produced top-notch linguists and pastor-scholars who could deal with the original texts of the Bible with great care and integrity. In fact, 'Geneva Academy succeeded in drawing students from many different countries, with the result that Calvinist scholars became some of the leading Christian Hebraists of the seventeenth century.'[35] The same can be said regarding the Academy's production of Christian scholars who dealt with the Greek text; they were exceptional for their day and age.

---

32 Walker, *John Calvin*, pp. 366-67.
33 I. L. Zabilka, 'Calvin's Contribution to Universal Education,' *ATJ* 44:1 (1989):90-91.
34 Ibid., p. 91.
35 Lloyd Jones, *The Discovery of Hebrew*, p. 79.

A good example of the linguistic prowess of the Genevan Academy is the succession of men who held the Hebrew chair during the sixteenth century. The first, as mentioned above, was Antoine Chevallier, who held the Hebrew chair until 1567 and then left the Academy for the chair in Hebrew studies at Cambridge University. His successor in Geneva was Corneille Bertram, a distinguished Hebraist, who published a comparative grammar of Hebrew and Aramaic (1574) while on faculty at Geneva. In 1587, Bertram was succeeded by Pierre Chevallier; he was not related to Antoine Chevallier, but he was one of his top students. The professorship in the final years of the sixteenth century was held by Jean Diodati (1576–1649). He was a brilliant linguist, and Beza recommended him for the Hebrew chair at the Academy when he was a mere twenty-one years of age! He had a singular, unique grasp of the oriental languages in his day. In addition, he translated the Bible into Italian in 1607.

Chapter Six

That Singular Instrument of God

An Ensign of the Reformation

Catholic priests and scholars of the sixteenth century were trained in Latin in order to use the Vulgate. Few of them, however, studied Greek and even fewer were trained and knowledgeable in Hebrew. What need was there to learn the languages to get at the real meaning of the Scriptures when, in fact, Jerome's Vulgate was the Bible of Christianity and the version upon which the Church of Rome based its doctrinal tenets and teachings? According to Lloyd Jones

> Ignorant and illiterate monks, alarmed by the progress of the new learning, thundered from the pulpit that a new language had been discovered called Greek, of which people should beware, since it was that which produced all the heresies. A book called the New Testament written in this language was now in everyone's hands, and was 'full of thorns and briers'. There was also another language called Hebrew, which should be avoided at all costs since those who learned it became Jews.[1]

---

1 Lloyd Jones, *The Discovery of Hebrew*, p. 26.

Although this view was commonplace in Catholicism prior to and during the early stages of the Reformation, it was not the only position held by Catholics. It was dominant, but not absolute. Johann Reuchlin, in particular, needs to be singled out. Indeed, he died as a member of the Roman Catholic Church in 1522, and he died adamantly opposed to Luther and the teaching of the Reformation. Reuchlin, however, prior to the Reformation made a strong and resounding case for the value of study of the original languages. In fact, in 1506, Reuchlin published his *De Rudimentis Hebraicis*, which really marked the beginning of Hebrew studies in Europe.[2]

And, of course, the work of Erasmus in the Greek language and his translation of the New Testament were absolutely ground-breaking. He did not want to abolish the use of the Vulgate in the Catholic Church, but he thought its meaning often to be unclear. He was convinced that his own translation directly from the original Greek made these meanings clear. This belief put him in a quandary: he did not wish to deviate from the teachings of the Church regarding the place of the Latin Vulgate, yet he believed the translation to be deficient and inferior.[3] Erasmus came under severe fire and criticism from the Catholic Church: he was roundly accused of condemning the authoritative version of the Bible approved by the Church and, thus, calling into question the very authority of the Church itself.

In contrast to the Roman Catholic Church, the Reformers were, for the most part, seriously committed to the study of the original languages of the Bible. It was a hall-mark of the Reformation. Among the reformers in this regard, Calvin did not stand alone. Luther, for example, had a very positive view toward the study of Greek and Hebrew throughout his life. He was convinced that a thorough study of them was an essential

---

2 W. Schwarz, *Principles and Problems of Biblical Translation* (Cambridge: Cambridge University Press, 1955), pp. 66-7.

3 Ibid., pp. 92-166.

part of the training of a theological student. In a letter he wrote to the Bohemian Brethren in 1523 regarding theological education he expresses his sympathies:

> And further, if I could bring it to pass among you I should like to ask that you do not neglect the languages but, since it would not be too difficult for you, that you have your preachers and some of your gifted boys learn Latin, Greek, and Hebrew well. I know for a fact that one who has to preach and expound the Scriptures and has no help from the Latin, Greek, and Hebrew languages, but must do it entirely on the basis of his mother tongue, will make many a pretty mistake. For it has been my experience that the languages are extraordinarily helpful for a clear understanding of the divine Scriptures.[4]

Luther often encouraged others in the study of the biblical languages. When Reuchlin, for example, came under heavy scrutiny by the Roman Catholic Church because of his efforts in Hebrew, Luther wrote him a letter of encouragement and commendation. He also was instrumental in the procurement of a Hebrew chair at the University of Wittenburg.[5]

Luther himself undertook the arduous task of learning both Greek and Hebrew. And his mastery of the two languages showed principally in his translation work of the Bible. He was an adequate exegete, that is, properly expounding the Scriptures based on the sane and sound historical-grammatical hermeneutic. He understood the biblical languages were a means to an end, namely, the proper exposition of Scripture. And he used them to that end. He said

> Even St. Augustine himself is obliged to confess, as he does in his *Christian Instruction*, that a Christian teacher who is to expound the Scriptures must know Greek and Hebrew in addition to

---

4 *Luther's Works*, vol. 36, ed. A. R. Wentz (Philadelphia: Fortress Press, 1955), p. 304.

5 W. H. Koenig, 'Luther as a Student of Hebrew,' *Concordia Theological Monthly* 24 (1953):849.

Latin. Otherwise it is impossible to avoid constant stumbling; indeed there are plenty of problems to work out even when one is well versed in the languages.[6]

Luther's friend and colleague Philipp Melanchthon (1497–1560) was appointed to the professorship of Greek at the University of Wittenberg at the young age of twenty-one (1518). He was a great promoter of the biblical languages, and he was proficient in Hebrew as well as in Greek. 'On his appointment as professor of Greek at Wittenburg in 1518 this promising young educator had delivered an inaugural address entitled *The Improvement of Studies* in which he challenged the obscurantists and called for the promotion of Latin, Greek and Hebrew within the university.'[7] He said in part:

> In theology, too, it is important how education is performed. If any field of studies, then theology requires especially talent, training, and conscientiousness.... But since the Bible is written in part in Hebrew and in part in Greek ... we drink from the stream of both – we must learn these languages, unless we want to be 'silent' persons as theologians. Once we understand the significance and weight of the words, the true meaning of Scripture will light up for us as the midday sun. Only if we have clearly understood the content ... if we put our minds to the [Greek and Hebrew] sources, we will begin to understand Christ rightly.[8]

Ulrich Zwingli promoted the study of the biblical languages by every means at his disposal. His views are clear in regard to a remark he made about the biblical Hebrew language: 'Ignorance of Hebrew forms of expression is responsible for many erroneous interpretations of Scriptural passages not only by ignorant and reckless men ... but also by genuinely

---

6 *Luther's Works*, vol. 45, pp. 362-3.
7 Lloyd Jones, *The Discovery of Hebrew*, p. 66.
8 H. J. Hillerbrand, ed. *The Reformation: A Narrative History Related by Contemporary Observers and Participants* (Grand Rapids: Baker, 1987), pp. 59-60.

pious and learned persons.' In fact, Zwingli was able to preach 'in Greek, Latin, and Hebrew with as much ease as in the vernacular,' a skill that earned Luther's jealousy![9]

Henry Bullinger provided a detailed description of a gathering at the Minster school in Zurich that was under the leadership of Zwingli. It occurred on June 19, 1525. He commented on the trilingual nature of the meeting:

> Mr. Ulrich Zwingli opened with a prayer.... Then one of the students read out so much of the lesson from the Bible as was to be expounded. This he read in Latin since the Bible was then translated into Latin.... After the student had read out the Latin, Jakob Ceporinus stood up and read the same passage again, this time in Hebrew, for the Old Testament was originally written in Hebrew, and he expounded the Hebrew in Latin. Then Zwingli read the same passage in Greek from the Septuagint and likewise expounded it in Latin showing the proper meaning and intent of any uncertain passages. Finally a preacher set out in German what had been said in the other languages, adding a prayer.[10]

When we consider the Reformation, it is usually characterized by the Latin expressions *sola scriptura, sola gratia,* and *sola fides*. And, indeed, these are principal teachings of the reformers and truths that we ought to hold to dearly. Yet, I would argue that the commitment of the reformers to the study of the original languages of the Bible was one of the hallmarks or emblems of the Reformation. It was the Reformation that gave the study of the biblical languages their true significance with a definite goal: to obtain a serious and impartial understanding of the Scriptures freed from the medieval hermeneutic. The church for centuries had been enslaved by the hermeneutic of allegory and church tradition.

---

9 Friedman, *The Most Ancient Testimony*, p. 257.
10 G. R. Potter, *Huldrych Zwingli* (New York: St. Martin's Press, 1978), p. 64. Taken from H. Bullinger, *Reformationsgeschichte nach dem Autographen*, vol. 1, eds. J. J. Hottinger and H. H. Vogeli (Frauenfeld, 1838–40), p. 290.

But the interpretive method of the Reformation was a single meaning to a text, and that meaning was the one intended by the author. In order to glean that sense, the student of the Bible must use a historical-grammatical approach to the Scriptures. An essential part of that task is to read and study the Word in its original tongues.

Reformed confessions

This commitment to the foundational nature of the biblical languages was reflected in many of the reformed confessions that soon followed the Reformation. As early as the Belgic Confession (1561) we read that God himself was the very author of the sacred Scriptures. And God was understood as the author of the Bible only in its original textual forms. Rohls accurately remarks that, 'Authenticity is attested for the canonical scriptures only in the original text, since only the original text has God as its author.'[11] The Westminster Confession of Faith (1642), for example, clearly underscores the invaluable and essential service that the biblical languages play in the life of the church because of God's inspiration of Scripture in those tongues. It says in Chapter I, Section VIII:

> The Old Testament in Hebrew (which was the native language of the people of God of old), and the New Testament in Greek (which at the time of writing of it was most generally known to the nations), being immediately inspired by God, and by his singular care and providence kept pure in all ages, are therefore authentical; so as in all controversies of religion the Church is finally to appeal unto them.

The Westminster Confession is stating that the final authority for solving disputations in the church is the Word of God in the *original text and tongue*, and that is what the

---

11 J. Rohls, *Reformed Confessions: Theology from Zurich to Barmen* (Louisville: Westminster/John Knox Press, 1998), p. 37.

church ought to appeal to.

The Second Helvetic Confession (1566) argues that the true and proper interpretation of Scripture is partially dependent on work in the original languages of the Bible. It says in Chapter II:5.010:

But we hold that interpretation of the Scripture to be orthodox and genuine which is gleaned from the Scripture themselves (from the nature of the language in which they were written, likewise according to the circumstances in which they were set down, and expounded in the light of like and unlike passages and of many and clearer passages) and which agree with the rule of faith and love, and contributes much to the glory of God and man's salvation.

The Geneva Bible

In 1553, Mary Tudor ascended to the throne of England. The new queen rigorously pursued a tie with the Roman Catholic Church and with the Catholicism of earlier centuries in Britain. She married the Roman Catholic Philip of Spain, and she was the catalyst for Parliament recognizing papal authority in England.[12] The public use of Bibles was then forbidden.[13] Persecution of Protestants resulted, and many of the gifted English Protestant scholars fled to Continental Europe. They sought refuge in many of the cities of the reformers, such as Basel, Zurich, Strassburg, and Frankfurt.

A good number of these scholars settled in Geneva, and they established an English church there in 1555. When these 'Marian' refugees arrived, 'John Calvin was daily expounding the Scriptures to scores of enthusiastic listeners. The emphasis

---

12 M. W. Anderson, 'The Geneva (Tomson/Junius) New Testament Among Other English Bibles of the Period,' in *The Geneva Bible*, ed. G. T. Sheppard (New York: Pilgrim Press, 1989), p. 5.

13 For a good survey of this period, see D. G. Danner, *The Theology of the Geneva Bible of 1560: A Study in English Protestantism* (Ann Arbor: University Microfilms, 1970).

was on making the Bible comprehensible, especially by means of vernacular versions.'[14] Geneva, at this time, was an important center for biblical textual scholarship. Beza was perhaps the best Bible scholar of the day in Europe, even surpassing Calvin himself. The leaders at Geneva welcomed the exiles with open arms, and their influence on the English scholars was clear and unmistakable.

The English Protestants had been using a translation called the 'Great Bible', which dated to 1539. In Geneva, the English refugees believed it was time to make another translation that would use most recent scholarship and one in which their theological positions and convictions would be presented. Thus, large portions of 'The Geneva Bible' were translated in Geneva, and many notes and annotations were added to aid in understanding the text. William Whittingham, one of the first translators, said that the purpose of the annotations was

> so that by this meanes both they which have not abilitie to by the Commentaries upon the Newe testament, and they also which have not opportunitie and leasure to reade them because of their prolixity may use this book in stede thereof...[15]

In this first edition of the Geneva Bible (1560), the notes reflect great influence of Calvin and, of course, the commonly held theological views of the Marian exiles. Later editions, such as the third edition (1602), appear to be more influenced by the work of Beza, which he accomplished after the death of Calvin.

The inclusion of commentary with text was an important step taken by the translators. Sheppard comments, 'The effect of the Geneva Bible was to safeguard the advance of the Reformation by placing text and commentary together.'[16]

---

14 Lloyd Jones, *The Discovery of Hebrew*, p. 127.
15 G. T. Sheppard, 'The Geneva Bible and English Commentary, 1600–1645,' in *The Geneva Bible*, ed. G. T. Sheppard (New York: Pilgrim Press, 1989), p. 1.
16 Ibid., p. 1.

The reality is, on the one hand, that the Geneva Bible maintained as its base literary core the translation of the Great Bible of 1539. Westcott, for example, argues that it was merely a revision of the Great Bible. He says:

> In all parts they took the Great Bible as their basis and corrected its text, without ever substituting for it a new translation. Even where the changes are greatest the original foundation can still be traced, and the new work fairly harmonizes with the old.[17]

On the other hand, the translators of the Geneva Bible, in numerous instances, were closer to the original Hebrew and Greek texts than their predecessors of the Great Bible. They were more competent to deal with difficult philological issues as well. Lloyd Jones comments: 'This is perhaps not surprising when we remember that the translation of 1560, in marked contrast to that of 1539, was the product of a team of scholars who could pool their resources when faced with a perplexing passage.'[18] And, indeed, no less a factor is the fact that much of the translation occurred in Geneva, a city which encouraged such work.

The Geneva Bible of 1560 had great influence and it was widely used in the English-speaking world. Beginning in 1558, the Marian exiles began to return to England due to the accession of Elizabeth I. These exiles brought back with them large portions of the Geneva Bible. After its first printing in 1560, the 'Geneva Bible became the most popular Bible in England and America and remained so until about 1640, when the less popular King James Version (1611) finally gained wide acceptance.'[19]

The Geneva Bible was not without its critics. King James,

---

17 B. F. Westcott, *A General View of the History of the English Bible* (New York: Macmillan, 1927), p. 222.
18 Lloyd Jones, *The Discovery of Hebrew*, p. 128.
19 Sheppard, 'The Geneva Bible,' p. 1.

at Hampton Court in 1604, attacked the commentary of the Geneva version, saying that it was the worst of all Bibles.[20] He attacked the use of the marginal notes by saying 'some notes very partiall, vntrue, seditious, and sauouring too much, of daungerous, and trayterous conceites.' He complained, in particular, about the notes in regard to Exodus 1:19 and 2 Chronicles 15:16. Both of these texts (and their comments) refer to how rulers are to be treated and obeyed. The King believed the comments gave entirely too much freedom and commendation to people for disobeying their ruler. Despite such objections, the Geneva Bible flourished among the people in the sixteenth and seventeenth centuries.

Education

Calvin's commitment to a trilingual education at the Geneva Academy had a deep and profound effect upon university education and scholarship throughout Europe. For example, 'Geneva Academy succeeded in drawing students from many different countries, with the result that Calvinist scholars became some of the leading Christian Hebraists of the seventeenth century.'[21] In 1597, a Genevan magistrate named Jacob Anjorrant was on a fund-raising mission in the Netherlands. He wrote back to Geneva regarding the reputation of the Academy in the Netherlands at the close of the sixteenth century. He said:

> Geneva still has a strong reputation, and the Dutch have noted that its reputation comes from the fact that through God's grace, for the last sixty-two years, pure religion has been preached there, without any sect or heresy appearing in the Academy. The Academy has flourished thanks to the reputation and worth of the outstanding people whose fame was and is known throughout the world, be it in theology, law, or in Hebrew, Greek and arts.

---

20 L. J. Trinterud, ed. *Elizabethan Puritanism* (New York: Oxford University Press, 1971), p. 206.
21 Lloyd Jones, *The Discovery of Hebrew*, p. 79.

Therefore, those who have had the opportunity to study under such professors are considered to be very learned. However, this would be of very little value if good discipline did not flourish as well. Geneva's reputation in this field is not small, because of the order and discipline that prevails there. As such, the young men who have spent time in Geneva are well thought of, as being well-trained, and because of this, they are placed more quickly in parishes. Therefore, it is Geneva's good discipline which leads fathers and guardians to send their children there, as many in the Low Countries have had to remove their children from France, Germany and England to send them there, confident in the high opinion which they have of Geneva.[22]

A prime example of Calvin's influence on European education in regard to the biblical languages was the founding of the University of Leiden in Holland. It was established in the 1570s, a few years after the death of Calvin. The school was formed on great Calvinistic leanings, and the founders made an unwavering pledge that the original languages of the Bible would be a central and important aspect of the curriculum.

Over fifty years after the creation of the university at Leiden, the great Hebrew scholar Sixtinus Amama wrote a book titled *Anti-Barbarus Biblicus* (1628). He dedicated the book to the Curators of the University of Leiden, along with the Committee of the States of Holland (that served approval for the founding of the university) and the mayors of Leiden. In his dedication, Amama

> reminds them of how fifty-seven years ago the States of Holland founded the University of Leiden in order to drive out barbarism, to protect the purified religion and to preserve the study of literature... In the foreword Amama explains the title *Anti-Barbarus Biblicus*. The barbarism which he is attacking is the neglect of Greek and

---

22 T. Heyer, 'Lettres-patentes des Provinces-Unies des Pays-Bas en faveur des Docteurs et autres gradués de l'Académie de Genève (1593 à 1599),' in *Mémories et Documents publiés par la Société d'Histoire et d'Archéologie de Genève* (1859), xi, pp. 161-92. Cited in Maag, *Seminary or University?*, p. 186.

Hebrew. The barbarians are those who can learn these languages but do not wish to do so. Amama wants to show how the neglect of Greek and Hebrew leads to a biblical barbarism and the decline of true religion. Such a depiction is necessary because even in the evangelical churches there are some who prefer to allegorise with Origen and Augustine rather than expound the Holy Scripture purely with Luther, Calvin and Bucer.[23]

This latter quotation is quite telling regarding the foundational principles of the university being in line with Calvin and the Geneva Academy. It is also revealing how quickly the University of Leiden drifted from those moorings, in particular, in its neglect of the biblical languages. Amama's remarks were an attempt to call the university back to its heritage and its founding purposes. The university had drifted from its original commitments, and it was having a great negative effect on the church and society in Holland.

Another example of Calvin's influence is that the 'academy was again the pattern for Emmanuel College at Cambridge.'[24] This college was founded in 1584 by Sir Walter Mildmay (1520–1589). Mildmay served as Chancellor of the Exchequer under Queen Elizabeth I, and he is well known for having been one of the commissioners in the trial of Mary Queen of Scots. He was a financier and philanthropist. And he was a staunch Calvinistic Puritan. His establishment of Emmanuel College at the University of Cambridge had the principal purpose to provide extensive theological training for Protestant preachers. The statutes of Emmanuel College reflect the purposes of the Geneva Academy: in addition to being 'professors of pure religion, contrary to Popery and other heresies' the students had to be 'skilled in the three tongues, Greek, Latin and Hebrew.' In fact, in order 'to maintain such high linguistic standards every

---

23 P. T. Van Rooden, *Theology, Biblical Scholarship and Rabbinical Studies in the Seventeenth Century* (Leiden: Brill, 1989), p. 68.
24 Zabilka, 'Calvin's Contribution,' p. 91.

candidate for a fellowship had to pass an examination in Greek and Hebrew before being admitted.'[25]

'The influence of Geneva was also apparent in the founding of the University of Edinburgh.'[26] This was Scotland's fourth university, and it had a post-Reformation origin. The university, like the Geneva Academy, 'was placed under the civil administration and the ministers of the city. This meant much more control of the curriculum and faculty. The university was intended to serve the Church.'[27] Although it did not begin to operate until 1583, the seeds of the school had been sown as early as 1560. At that time, Edward Henderson was appointed to 'teiche and reid within the burgh of Edinburgh ane publict lessoun in the lawis and ane uther in Greik thryis in the oulk.'[28] Even at that most primitive stage the languages played a most foundational part in the education.

* * * * *

Calvin firmly believed in an educated pastorate, and part of this *eruditio* was mastery of the languages of Scripture. Prudence and fairness requires us to agree with the assessment of David Puckett when he concludes that Calvin 'probably should not be regarded as a expert Hebraist, as was Münster, but he did know the language a great deal better than the seventeenth-century Roman Catholic scholar Richard Simon believed.'[29] Basil Hall perhaps provides an accurate judgment when he says that Calvin was 'competent in Hebrew without being a distinguished Hebraist' and that he was an '*homme trilingue*, a worthy representative of French biblical humanism.'[30] The reality is that 'there is scarcely a Reformed exegete of the

---

25 Lloyd Jones, *The Discovery of Hebrew*, p. 145.
26 Zabilka, 'Calvin's Contribution,' p. 91.
27 Ibid., p. 91.
28 G. Donaldson, *Scotland: James V–James VII*, vol. 3 (Edinburgh: Oliver and Boyd, 1965), p. 267.
29 Puckett, *John Calvin's Exegesis*, p. 58.
30 B. Hall, 'Biblical Scholarship: Editions and Commentaries,' in *The Cambridge*

sixteenth century who did not have a good knowledge of Hebrew and was passionately concerned to establish the *hebraica veritas*.'[31] Calvin was an excellent Greek scholar, yet, again, he was not alone. Indeed, Reformed interpreters of the sixteenth century were masters of the Greek language, and men like Beza even surpassed Calvin in it.

It is not Calvin's personal ascendancy as a biblical linguist that sets him apart in the sixteenth century. That is not his legacy in regard to the biblical languages. Knox called Calvin 'that singular instrument of God.' And, indeed, the appropriate word to define Calvin's linguistic legacy is *instrumentality*. He may not have been the greatest biblical linguist of his day, but he was certainly a primary driving force in promoting Greek and Hebrew as essential to the correct interpretation of the Bible. In this regard, he laid much of the groundwork for proper Reformed exegesis. In addition, he produced a body of pastor-scholars, who were competent in Greek and Hebrew, and he sent them into the world to affect it with the very truth and power of the Word of God. The latter may in fact be his crowning work and his legacy – for it is one that remains to this very day.

History of the Bible, vol. 3, ed. S. L. Greenslade (Cambridge: Cambridge University Press, 1963), p. 89.

31 Kraus, 'Calvin's Exegetical Principles,' p. 15.

Postscript: A Plea

The Problem

The Reformed community today is an heir of the Reformation's linguistic heritage. I fear, however, that we are adrift today and, indeed, even more acutely than any time in history. Many Protestant and Evangelical seminaries do not require the biblical languages for the divinity degree, and many do not teach them at all, especially as regards the language of Hebrew. Some theological schools have retreated to the point of teaching the biblical languages on-line or simply offering a 'tools' approach. It appears to be rare that preachers use Hebrew in their study of an Old Testament text, no matter using it in sermon preparation. The same holds true for Greek, although perhaps not to the same degree. In 1903, William Robertson Nicoll wrote a letter to James Denney about pastoral education, and it reflects the sentiments of many in Evangelicalism for the past century:

> While I hold strongly that there ought to be a good portion of ministers with a good theological education, knowing Hebrew and Greek and so forth, I feel it is wasted on many. What good

is Hebrew to the majority of ministers? Even in the Presbyterian churches they never open a Hebrew Bible from one year's end to the other. I should like to see our students taught to read English, to know what English means, which only a small majority do.

This is not an uncommon view. Richard Watson accurately reflects these sentiments when he says:

> Some seminary students spend a tremendous amount of time studying Hebrew, but in a small survey of pastors who have been in the ministry for ten years or more, not one still used Hebrew. Most of them reported that they gave it up immediately after completing the last required course. This is not a new discovery but has been a source of jokes among pastors for years. Why, then, have seminaries not changed the Hebrew program to make it useful or otherwise eliminate it entirely?[1]

Watson's base point in his article is that seminaries ought to consider reducing requirements in biblical languages while expanding those in more practical subjects such as human relations, personnel management, and communication.[2] Today this type of logic is common. In reality, it is utilitarianism and pragmatism at its best.

What lies behind this movement is complex. I will mention only two of many reasons why biblical languages are often being shunned today. First, it demonstrates a movement toward professional training rather than academic achievement.[3] It reflects a trade-school mentality, and a closet anti-intellectualism. Second, the movement mirrors the pragmatic temper of western society. If there is no immediate relevance, gratification, or application, then how valuable can

---

1 R. G. Watson, 'Secularists Did Not Steal the Colleges,' *Presbyterian Journal* 45:3 (1986):8-10.

2 See the response by D. E. Johnson, 'The Peril of Pastors Without the Biblical Languages,' *Presbyterian Journal* 45:7 (1986):23-24.

3 E. E. Ellis, 'Language Skills and Christian Ministry,' *Reformed Review* 24:3 (1971):162-63.

it be? Hafemann goes as far as to argue that one of the reasons for the dismissal of the relevance of biblical languages is the influence of post-modernism.[4]

But there is grave danger here. First and foremost, the neglect of the original languages is a movement away from the centrality of the Scriptures in our churches and away from the pastor's main duty to teach the Scriptures. Historically in Reformed circles the primary duty of the pastor was to preach from the Bible, to teach from the Bible, to encourage and edify from the Bible, and so forth. Scripture was the core of the pastoral ministry. And too often that does not seem to be the case today: a minister now is an administrator, a counselor, a programmer, and a veritable CEO. He is to perform whatever his congregation expects of him. The Bible then is relegated to being merely another resource of ministry. And that is shameful.

The case for the biblical languages

> The languages are the sheath containing the sword of the Spirit
> (Martin Luther).

Why should ministry students and pastors study Greek and Hebrew? Here I will present some of the most important reasons why knowledge of the biblical languages is necessary and *practical* in the ministry.

1. The Holy Scriptures were revealed by God through his prophets in Greek and Hebrew (and Aramaic). Why would the pastor as interpreter not want to study God's Word in its original linguistic revelation and form? Do you not think that the reader of Shakespeare would be better off knowing Middle English? In the study of Homer, would it not be most valuable to know classical Greek? The truth is that without the original languages a student's skill to examine a text in its own context,

---

[4] S. Hafemann, *2 Corinthians* (Grand Rapids: Zondervan, 2000), pp. 171-73.

biblical text or extra-biblical text, is severely crippled.

2. There is an abundance of English translations of the Bible. Some of them are solid and good, but as Waltke points out with an Italian proverb, 'Traduttore tradittore,' 'translations are treacherous.'[5] How does a pastor know which is the best translation of a text without knowing how to translate? Congregations are curious about matters of translation and they want to know and use the best. The pastor needs to be capable of guiding his flock in these matters.

3. There are many excellent commentaries on the market today. The pastor often thinks that because there are so many that the labor has been done, and he need not go over well-furrowed ground. Hafemann discerningly responds: 'It is precisely because there are so many excellent commentaries available today that the use of the biblical languages in preaching becomes more important, not less.'[6] The proliferation of commentaries means a proliferation of opinions, views, and interpretations of the text. How does a student or a pastor judge what is right? Without the languages the pastor's ability to examine commentaries and to discern what is good and true is severely hampered.

4. Ability in the biblical languages aids in refuting false teaching. The Westminster Confession of Faith says that 'in all controversies of religion the Church is finally to appeal unto them,' namely, the Holy Scriptures in the original languages that were 'immediately inspired by God' (Chapter I, Section VIII). Johnson points out that the knowledge of Greek and Hebrew is especially beneficial for one 'to be able to respond to the bogus appeals to "the original" by false teachers.'[7] The biblical languages are a sword to be unsheathed against heresy and false teaching.

---

5 B. K. Waltke, 'How I Changed My Mind About Teaching Hebrew (or Retained it),' *Crux* 29:4 (1993):10-15.

6 S. Hafemann, 'Why Use Biblical Languages in Preaching?' *Southern Baptist Journal of Theology* 3 (1999):86-89.

7 Johnson, 'The Perils of Pastors,' p. 23.

5. It can not be proven that there is no difference between a prepared, studious sermon based on the biblical languages and one that is not. Preachers today often proudly say that they never make use of the language skills they acquired in seminary – having heard some of them preach, I have no doubt that they are telling the truth! The reality is that when one wrestles with the text and has direct contact with the Word of God in the languages in which it was revealed, a certain depth and richness pervades the study, one that would not have been there otherwise. And, indeed, there is 'a freshness about his preaching that derives from his direct contact with the Word.'[8]

6. It is true that the maintaining of and the use of the biblical languages throughout time and ministry requires diligence and discipline. It may be difficult to do, but the rewards can be immense. For these labors foster discipline, depth of character, commitment, and conviction in ministry. The work leads to solid, accurate, and fresh preaching and teaching. Pastors have been called to guard the sacred deposit and stand against any misuse: this may be hard and strenuous work. The biblical languages are one of the weapons that we have been supplied with to make such a stand.

There are many other reasons why Greek and Hebrew are necessary, central, and foundational to ministry. I refer the reader to literature in the area.[9] I would, however, briefly mention one further reason, and it is apropos to what we have been discussing in this book. With the neglect of the biblical languages we are in jeopardy of losing a distinctive characteristic of the Reformation and of our reformational

---

8 Ibid., p. 24.
9 See, for example, E. C. Brisson, 'Let Down Your Nets! A Case for Biblical Languages,' *As I See It Today* (1995):1-4; D. Doriani, 'A Pastor's Advice on Maintaining Original Language Skills,' *Presbyterion* 19:2 (1993):103-15; and S. Hafemann, 'Seminary, Subjectivity, and the Centrality of Scripture: Reflections on the Current Crisis in Evangelical Seminary Education,' *Journal of the Evangelical Theological Society* 31 (1988):129-43.

heritage. And that, indeed, would be a travesty. We need pastor-scholars, men like Calvin and those whom he trained, to stand up and guard the sacred deposit that has been left to our charge. We have been left a wonderful legacy, but one question yet remains: what will we in the reformed community today do with that legacy?

Appendix:
A Sermon of John Calvin on Deuteronomy 16:1-4

I have included a sermon of John Calvin on Deuteronomy 16:1-4 as an illustration of his preaching style. A few words on the translation that I have used are in order. First, I did not use a new translation of the sermon from French into English. The reason for that is that I believe that a reliable translation already exists, so why reinvent the wheel? The translation that I employ is that made by Arthur Golding (1536–1605). Golding finished his translation of all of Calvin's sermons on the Book of Deuteronomy and wrote a preface to the work in the year of 1582. It was then published in 1583. I have not, however, merely provided a facsimile of Golding's translation of the present sermon, although it is available.[1] I have attempted to provide an updating of the sermon for more modern English ears. There are numerous archaisms that I have tried to make readable and understandable. Yet, I have also tried not to destroy or alter the integrity of the translation of Golding.

---

1 See J. Calvin, *Sermons on Deuteronomy* (Edinburgh: Banner of Truth, 1987). This is a facsimile edition of the original publication by H. Middleton in London in 1583.

Golding was of the day and age of Calvin, and perhaps he understood much better than we many of the historical and literary contexts of the sermon.

Golding was an excellent English translator. He is perhaps best known for his translation of Ovid's *Metamorphoses* (1567). Marlowe, Spenser, and even Shakespeare used his translation of Ovid.[2] Golding also translated Calvin's commentaries on the Psalms (1571) and his sermons on Job, Galatians, and Ephesians. He held strong Calvinistic and Puritan sympathies and, therefore, he had keen theological discernment and understanding for his task at hand.

A few words in regard to the nature of this sermon are in order. Calvin's preaching of this sermon is first and foremost *theological*. In it, although he deals primarily with the Passover, he presents a basic sacramental theology. The sermon is *Christological*, that is, it is Christ-centered preaching. Calvin views the Passover as a mere shadow and type of the coming Messiah, the lamb of God, who will lay down his life for his people. It is *polemical*. What I mean by that word is that the tone of Calvin's exposition is highly contentious; he strongly disputes the teachings of Catholicism in regard to the sacraments. He is not hesitant to use volatile language in denying the validity of Catholic thought. The sermon is *pedagogic* and *didactic*. Calvin is clearly interested in the instruction of the people through his preaching. This preaching has many other attributes, but I will mention only one other: it is *linguistic*. In two points of the sermon, Calvin demonstrates his knowledge of the Hebrew language. I encourage the reader to pay close attention to those examples.

All of these characteristics of the sermon find their *telos* in the final paragraph of the sermon. There the exposition reaches a crescendo in the glorification of the majestic God of Israel and the Church. There Calvin presents the gospel message:

---

2 See A. Golding (trans.), M. Forey, ed. *Ovid's Metamorphoses* (Baltimore: Johns Hopkins University Press, 2002).

that Jesus Christ came to save sinners, and those whom he has saved 'he plucked out of the gulf of death'. Calvin's message is ultimately one of grace.

On Tuesday the fifth of November. 1555.

> The XCvii. Sermon which is the first upon the Sixteenth Chapter.
>
> *1 You shall keep the month of new fruits, that you may keep the Passover to the Lord your God. For in the month of new fruits the Lord your God brought you out of the land of Egypt.*
>
> *2 And you shall sacrifice the Passover to the Lord your God, even sheep and oxen, in the place which the Lord your God will choose to put his name there.*
>
> *3 You shall eat no leavened bread in that feast: seven days you shall eat unleavened bread, even the bread of sorrow. For you came in haste out of the land of Egypt: to the end be mindful of the day of your departure out of the land of Egypt all the days of your life.*
>
> *4 And there no leaven shall be seen in your house, during the seven days in all your coasts. Also you shall not leave of the flesh that is sacrificed from the evening of the former day till the next morning.*

This present chapter treats the three feasts which God ordained among the Jews: that is, the feast of Easter or Passover, the feast of Pentecost or Whitsuntide, and the feast of Tabernacles or Tents. First he treats the Passover, and God ordains that it should be diligently observed: for it was a memorial of great importance, whereby the people were put in mind, how they had been redeemed, and put in possession of the inheritance that had been promised unto them. It was profitable that the same should be known: for it was the foundation of all the benefits which the Jews had received at God's hands, and which they looked for afterwards. Without that, they would have been no people separated and dedicated to God, neither had they any hope of salvation: for the covenant made with their fathers would have been defeated. Therefore it is not without cause, that God would have that day kept holy, and with such ceremony. In the same way it was with the feast of Tabernacles, as we shall see later. For it served to put the Jews in mind of their going out of Egypt, and that whereas they had dwelt a long time in the wilderness, without house or home, and yet God had ever preserved them: it profited them likewise to acknowledge the same benefit. But we will treat every feast in its due order.

Presently we have to speak of the Passover. But before I go any further, we must mark also that God respected not only what he had done already, but also meant with it that there should be a figure of things to come, whereof we have the truth and substance, since the time that our Lord Jesus Christ has been discovered to the world. That is why Saint Paul tells the Colossians that these things were but shadows, the body is in Christ Jesus. True it is that he speaks not there expressly of Easter by name: but yet under the name of Sabbath, he comprehends all the feasts, and likewise all the ceremonies that depended upon them. To be short, God had a double purpose in ordaining the Passover. The one was to make the people of Israel to understand, that they came not into possession of that land of Canaan by their own power: but that they had been led there by the hand of God. And because they had been delivered by miracle out of the land of Egypt; God's will was that the same should be declared. Again, for as much as the same deliverance was a figure of the deliverance that was to be hoped for by our Lord Jesus Christ: this feast of Passover extended yet further, that is, that when the people ate of the paschal lamb (as they called it) they should think thus within themselves: This is a shadow and figure of the sacrifice which shall be once offered up, whereby the world shall be reconciled and set free. And although the thing was not yet apparent to the eye, yet it was profitable to the faithful to inure themselves to the hope of the redeemer who God had promised them. And in that respect, Saint Paul says in the first letter to the Corinthians, that Jesus Christ is our Passover or paschal lamb, and that he is sacrificed for us, and that we must now eat of that sacrifice: albeit not with the leaven of malice and deceitfulness, but with righteousness and soundness. That is the one point which we have to remember.

And that the paschal lamb was not a bare ceremony without doctrine; it appears by that which is written in the twelfth chapter of Exodus, where it is said, that when the sacrificed lamb is being eaten, if their children ask what it means, their fathers shall answer: the Lord brought us out of the land of Egypt where we were in bondage, and therefore we will do this thing yearly in remembrance thereof: not that the doing thereof one day only may discharge us: but that the same should continue printed in our hearts, so as in enjoying the land of Canaan, we may understand that we conquered it not by our own strength, but through his good pleasure, because it was his will to harbor us here, according to that promise which he has made to our forefathers. We see then how the feast of Passover was not a ceremony without instruction, but that it contained doctrine in it. And it is an article of great importance. For the world would always have a great number of ceremonies to no purpose; and in the mean it seems enough to have a store of gay shows. But to the contrary, God tells us that ceremonies are toys and trifles, unless they lead us further, and promise us things concerning our salvation, so as we be taught and confirmed in the faith by means of them. If that not be in them, they be stark baggage, and worth nothing. No, they be nothing else than a corrupting of that service of God, and the high way to lead us to superstition and idolatry. As for example, we see how they make a great number of disguisings in Popedome: but in the mean they knew not what any of these things mean. If you come to their masse, there they play an interlude, where there are as many fond toys as can be. Indeed, the wretched world ravishes at them: but that is because they know nothing, but are utterly sotted, and yet they bear themselves in hand that they have done a good deed, and that God ought to like it very well, when they have so bestirred themselves. But (as I told you before) they be but vain and fond apish toys. And why so? For God never meant to ordain any ceremonies among his people, which contained not some good instruction, and served not to some good end. And, therefore, let us mark well, that whereas the Jews had that feast of Passover, they had God's word also, whereby they were warranted that it was not invented at the pleasure of men. For God not only gave a prefixed commandment saying: you shall observe such a day: but also a doctrine with it, and willed that the fathers should teach it to their children, and put them in remembrance of the deliverance that had been made, as indeed it was as excellent a deed as might be. That then was of his appointment.

And so let us bear in mind, that if we nowadays have ceremonies without instruction, they shall all be condemned by God, who utterly dislikes them, and we can not allege them to be of his service. For he declares and avows it to be but foolish superstition, when men turn away from that mark, and that it is the next way to put us quite besides our salvation. And herein we defy all the huge heap of pomps wherein the papists serve God: for there is nothing in them that God avows. Also we be warned to mingle nothing with the pure simplicity of the sacraments and ceremonies which God would have to be observed nowadays. Let us be content with that which is shown to us: for if we add never so little to it, surely we shall make such a minglemangle as will be nothing worthwhile, after the manner of the papists, who (as we see) have invented many things out of their own head. We must have this and that, they say, why so? To what purpose? O (say they) it will serve for such a thing: but in the meantime there is no instruction toward God. Is it their part to cause a doctrine to be brought in? It is right that God should speak. And when men hear him, then every one shall be edified. But when men thrust themselves in, and fall to forging fond devotions without authority from God, all must be cast down. The world sees how the papists have corrupted the true sacraments. In baptism, the water has been esteemed as nothing in the Popedome: for it is no matter if the infants [pisse in it]. But as for the holy cream that is in it, O, it is not for any man to touch that: for that is too heavenly a thing. And, yet, notwithstanding the water is the substance of that sacrament, and the whole perfection thereof. But as for the cream, who deified it? It is a stinking grace that men have charmed, and blowed upon, like sorcerers. And should that be had in such reverence, that the sacrament which proceeds from the son of God, should be had in no estimation for it? Moreover, the water (by their reckoning) is not good, unless it has been conjured, and that a number of charms have been made over it, to amaze the ignorant. And therefore so much the better ought we to bear this lesson in mind, that we may be fenced against all Satan's inventions; which is, that we would see our minds as so ticklish, that we would happily invent some new thing, and we bear ourselves in hand that we have spun a fair thread, when some new ceremony comes forth by our means: it stands us in hand to think thusly, yes, but God despises all this gear, yes, and he shows us that we do but pervert his service, when we add anything after that fashion of our own. Then it is an infallible doctrine that no ceremonies are profitable or to be made account of among the faithful, unless they carry instruction with them. And that instruction must come of God: for it is his office to teach us, he reserves that authority to himself. And, therefore, it is to be concluded that the ceremonies which are set forth by men, are but trifles and trinkets, even with how great a show of wisdom there seems to be in them.

And hereby we see also that it was superstitiously done of such as bear the name of Christians, to bring in a feast of Passover under pretense that the Jews had it: for the aspects are very diverse. I mean not that we may not have one day in the year, in which to celebrate the remembrance of the resurrection of our Lord Jesus Christ: for we must not run so rigorously into extremes, as that our infirmity might not have some help, to quicken it, that we might better think all of our life, what benefit the rising again of our Lord Jesus Christ has brought to us. Well then may we have a day appointed to that purpose for orders sake: but to make a service of God thereof, or to think that we ought to fashion ourselves after the example of the Jews; that as they had their Passovers, so ought we too: it is an abuse that tends to turn all things upside down, and a putting of a veil before the face of Jesus Christ, that men might not know the light of the gospel. These things (as I said) were but shadows, which we now have as the body and substance: and therefore it is a hiding of Jesus Christ, when men bring in feasts after the manner of the Jews.

But now let us come to that which is commanded here concerning the Easterday of the Jews. *You shall eat unleavened bread or cakes (says he) by the space of six days, and there shall no leavened bread be found in your houses.* This was done because the Jews departed in haste out of the land of Egypt. And it ought to have made them think that they did not go out with banners displayed, as though their enemies stood in fear of them and did not dare to complain against them: for they went away like a sort of poor fugitives. The women carried their children upon their shoulders, the men took up their stuff in their necks, and quickly fled away; and their enemies would have pursued them, and they were of strength and power enough to have done it. The Jews on the other side were a people that had no skill to handle a sword: for they had been held in such slavery, that they did not once look upon a sword or any weapon of war. They had been used like asses and oxen. Their fate had been as slavish as could be. Well then, when the time came that they should depart, it was said to them, you get out. And what bread shall we have to eat? What provision shall there be by the way? Grind your corn, and gather it up quickly in meal upon your shoulders, and as the time will serve you shall bake it by the way and eat it. Now when the people had this solemn rite yearly, wherein they ate cakes without leaven, it served to put them in mind, that when their fathers departed out of Egypt, they were a poor fugitive people that ran away like a lamb that is pursued by wolves. You see in what plight they were. It must therefore be concluded that God had preserved them after a wonderful fashion. For what were the Egyptians? A nation full of pride and cruelty. A mighty nation, a nation that trusted in their own force and power; and, moreover, a nation that bore deadly hatred to the poor Jews, an utter enemy to them, and such a one that desired nothing so much as to root out that remembrance of them, as the tyranny of Pharaoh well showed. Now then the Jews were put in mind that God had made them escape out of their enemies' hands, so as they could not but know that they had been helped by him, and that the prayer of their life was to be yielded unto him. As if they should say, You Lord have delivered us, not only from that state of bondage but also as it were by fetching us out of our graves. For we were as it were stark dead, and had been past all hope of recovery, if you had not reached us with your mighty arm. That was the thing in which the Jews were put in mind, when God commanded them to eat unleavened bread. And it was his will that this should be done, not only that same night that they ate the Passover lamb, but also that same ceremony should be continued by the space of six days together. And why? God showed thusly that men are not thoroughly shaped to the doctrine that he sets down to them, though the same is clear enough. Does God speak? There is no darkness in his speech. But, yet, the case stands, we can not fasten upon it. For we are so slow minded that we can never attain to his meaning, until he has repeated our lesson to us diverse times. That is why he commanded expressly that they should eat unleavened bread by the space of six days together. As if he should say, truly the one night's eating of the paschal lamb with unleavened bread, ought to be a sufficient instruction to you what is meant by the same. But what? I see well that you are shortwitted, insomuch that if you have heard any thing from God's mouth, you forget it out of hand. And therefore when I intend to teach you, I must deal with you as it were by measure and compass. And therefore if you have a good long time before hand to think of the eating of the paschal lamb, you will be better prepared unto it. Therefore shall you have a whole week, wherein you shall eat no leavened bread; by means thereof you shall be quickened to think upon the great and inestimable benefit which God bestowed upon your fathers in delivering them out of the land of Egypt, so as you may bear well in mind that his delivering of them was after a strange manner, and that he desired to work after a heavenly manner, because you were in such a wretched plight, that you may have seemed to be already swallowed up in death, and to have been already buried in your graves. Now we see why the Jews were expressly commanded to abstain from the eating of leavened bread.

There were other ceremonies also; that is to wit, the girding up of their garments, the putting on of their shoes, and the taking of their walking staves in their hands. For in those eastern countries they wore long garments after the same manner that the Turks do at this day. And when they traveled by the way, they tied up their garments about their loins, as the gray Friars and Jacobines or white Friars do and such others that are so greatly encumbered by clothes. Now God made the Jews to understand that they should be as wayfarers when they ate the paschal lamb, and that they should eat it in haste, to put them in remembrance of the said departure out of Egypt. And our Lord did set down this figure as a looking glass for the Jews to behold how their forefathers ate the paschal lamb, even when they were quick to go their ways, that they might acknowledge so great a benefit. And herein we see how God had a concern for the ignorance of his people, as indeed all the ceremonies we serve in our infirmity. What does baptism or the Lord's supper bring us? Do they make the death and passion of our Lord Jesus Christ of more value than it is of itself? What help do we find in the bread, or in the wine, or in the water, to that purpose? God's purpose then was not to add anything to that which we have received in our Lord Jesus Christ, but to bear with our ignorance because he sees us to be unable to comprehend the things that are gotten for us by our Lord Jesus Christ. For inasmuch as they be too high for us, God helps us up to them by the outward and visible signs which we have in those sacraments. But it profited the Jews to have more such helps than we. For they had not so plain a doctrine as is now contained in the Gospel. Again, Jesus Christ was not yet come, in whom we see all that ever can be wished for in regard to salvation. The heavens were then opened to us, when his side was opened to wash us clean, and his body offered up for a sufficient sacrifice to reconcile us to God his father, and to do away with all our offenses and transgressions. When these things were done, then we had a full warrant of our salvation. Therefore, in these days, we need not to be helped with so huge a heap of ceremonies as had the ancient fathers under the law. It is enough that we be led to our Lord Jesus Christ, in which few signs are necessary, that is, baptism and the Lord's supper. For seeing that the son of God is content with those two, we also ought to rest therein. Nevertheless, we see here how God vouchsafed to stoop to the infirmity of his people, by giving them a lively representation of their departing out of the land of Egypt, and by setting them down, as it were, in a looking glass or painted table, for them to behold how he had delivered them: that is, like a sort of poor people that were taking their journey to flee away secretly, and were so distressed that they could not turn to face so mighty enemies, who were able to swallow them up at the first chop without any resistance. Seeing then that the Jews had such instruction, they should have thought to themselves: how did it come to pass that we are alive this day, but that our God has preserved us? And how is it that we stand but only by his mere mercy? For we would have perished if he had not reached out his arm to bring us out of the land of Egypt. Thus much concerning this point.

Now it was commanded further, that the paschal lamb should be eaten with bitter herbs. And our Lord himself speaks here expressly of the bread of sorrow: as if he had said, although you eat the paschal lamb in rest, and when you come to the enjoyment of the inheritance I have promised you, you must have a memorial of the anguish in which your fathers were, and you must think that without my favor you should have had neither paschal lamb nor a bit of bread to eat this day; for you should have been utterly rooted out of the world. Consider it, therefore, and that you be better moved by it, take bitter herbs, that is to say, abstain from all the delicious in your eating of the paschal lamb. For the Jews were not restrained from taking their repast after their eating of the paschal lamb, as we see that our Lord Jesus Christ in eating of the paschal lamb with his disciples, insomuch as they did not only sit down at a table, but also lay down after the old manner, which was to eat their meals lying half to one side. Certain it is that he kept the law to the uttermost, for he submitted himself to it to set us free from it. Then we must note that our Lord ate the paschal lamb after the same manner that was ordained by Moses, that is, standing upon his feet, with his staff in his hand, and his shoes on his feet, and having his loins girded up like a wayfarer. And after this was done he took his accustomed repast, for this was a solemn sacrifice, and therefore we must not wonder that it was separated from the common meats; for it was necessary that all the folks of one house ate thereof, so as if there were thirty or forty persons in a house, every man had his portion of it. And if the household was not great enough, two or three households were called together and they met in one place, so that the sacrifice might be eaten up quickly. A lamb was roasted in haste and eaten with a morsel of sweet cake; yes and they were forbidden to boil it, to show that they could have no leasure to tarry till it was half boiled, but they were to devour it hastily [like folke that were to go their waies out of hand]. But however the case stood, it profited them to eat it with bitter herbs. Whereby we are to understand, that delicious things do keep us from the due consideration of God's benefits, to be ravished by them. For although it has been said, You shall be joyful before your God; yet we are continually held back in this world, when we have some allurement to withdraw us from God. For if our flesh has her desires, then we are overtaken by such things, that we stay not aloft to behold well the spiritual grace of God. Thus you see why the bitter herbs were put to the sacrifice so as to make men consider the better after what manner the people had been delivered, being in such extreme anguish as they were not able to endure anymore.

Besides this they were also forbidden to admit any heathen man to it, unless he were circumcised. True it is that God commanded that the servants being born strangers should eat of it. Yes, but that was not before they were first incorporated into his Church by receiving the sign of circumcision. Here we are to understand that it was a peculiar token given by God to his own people. For sacraments are peculiar to the Church. They are not things for men to put to unholy use, nor to leave as an undertaking for all men. For our Lord will have us to be gathered together under his name. When we use the sacraments, let us think thus about ourselves, behold here is a treasure that God has kept and laid up for us as for his children. And, indeed, if a man should nowadays admit as many to the Lord's supper as would offer to come to it, would it not be a defiling of Scripture? And yet there are a number to be seen who would have all men indifferently, both rag and tag, to be admitted to it; but such people never yet know how to use the sacraments rightly. For (as we shall declare hereafter) the Supper of our Lord Jesus Christ is to us today the same that the paschal lamb was to the people of the Jews. Wherefore let us mark in a few words how our Lord has showed this sacrament as a warrant given by him to his people, that he took them to be his Church, and therefore that it ought not to be set forth as an undertaking for all comers. True it is that circumcision likewise was a sacrament, but there was a diversity of aspects between the one and the other. For by circumcision, people were received into the number of God's people, so as it was an entrance into the Church as baptism is this day; by means whereof such as by nature are not numbered in that company of God's children, are received and incorporated into them by baptism. And so stood the case with those Jews for circumcision. But as for the paschal lamb, that was to be kept to the Jews themselves.

Now it is also said, *that it was not to be eaten throughout the whole country; but that it was to be done in the place which the Lord had chosen to put his name in.* And truly this was not shown to them on the first day, insomuch that they had been a long time in the land of Canaan, before the Ark had any certain resting place, there was no such place assigned to it. But yet it profited them always to be obedient to the ceremony of resorting to that place where the Ark was, until Mount Zion was marked out. And then all men were bound to repair there, each from the uttermost borders of the country. All men were to come to Jerusalem, except they be hindered by sickness or old age. And why? It was not to give a precedent for the Pilgrimages which the Papists invented afterward; for in so doing they showed themselves to differ nothing at all from the Jews. Again, it is not for them to excuse themselves by the example of the Jews, for the Jews had a commandment of God, but the Papists made their vagaries for their own pleasure, wherein they utterly renounced Jesus Christ and overthrew that which is said in the fourth chapter of Saint John, namely, that the time was come that God would be no more worshipped in any certain place, but would have his name called upon everywhere throughout the whole world. Besides this, we must mark that there was a special reason why God would have the Jews to resort to Jerusalem to sacrifice the paschal lamb there, namely, to the end that no man should attempt to alter anything in that order which he had set by the Law. And (as I have said) this ancient ceremony was a thing of great importance, in which the people were informed of their Redeemer, even that he had brought them out of the land of Egypt, and that he would send them yet another redeemer, by whom the whole world should be redeemed. Lo, here is a ceremony that imported a wonderful secret and therefore it was right that it should be kept purely. For in doing it, God called all the Jews into one body, that having the sanctuary and the temple before their eyes, they might better put in mind that it was not lawful for them to add anything at their own pleasure, but that it profited them to follow that common doctrine, to understand that God represented himself there, and dwelt among them by means of the Ark. Seeing then that the people were so gathered together, they could not but be restrained from starting out into foolish intentions; and the doctrine needs to be retained, as I have said before, for that ceremony was nothing of itself, it had been but as a May game or a mockery. That was why the people were drawn to Jerusalem, as to that place which God had appointed. And so we see now why it was said that they should not do sacrifice in any of their cities or towns, but assemble all together in the city of Jerusalem.

It is enjoined further that they should not break a bone of the paschal lamb. And why so? As if it were said that it was meat to be eaten in haste (as I have already shown) so as they were forbidden to boil any part of it. And hereby God meant to show even better that haste which the people made in departing out of that land of Egypt; for it was not for them to set the pot upon the fire to boil it, for they would never have had time to do it. Therefore they were to make haste and to eat this lamb half roasted, as people pressed upon by their enemies, and as people that looked to have been overtaken every minute of the hour. By reason therefore they had no leisure to stand gnawing on the bones, or to break them to get out the marrow, as people do when they have time. They could do none of this, but they were to eat that sacrifice in haste, and to cast away the rest. We see then as now, that concerning the deliverance that had already been done, things were as pointed out with the finger in the paschal lamb. And for this cause, the very term itself is expressed here, for the Hebrew word *Passah* is the same that we call *Passing* in English. And by that word our Lord confirmed that thing of which we have spoken before, namely, that this ceremony was not a fond device to busy men's heads as though they were little babies, but that it imports instruction to edify people to the end that they should think thusly: this day must we pay homage to our God for our life, because he preserved us by his own infinite goodness, by bringing us out of the land of Egypt. So then God did not simply speak of those things that ought to be observed, but his meaning was to show his wisdom in such a way as that people might consider, we have made a passage; and what manner of a passage? Even such a one as we who have no legs to go, but God did lift us up by his power and made us to pass over it as a gulf of death, not only in passing the Red Sea, but also when we were yet in Egypt. For before we came to the Red Sea, there was another strait to pass, which we should never have escaped if God had not opened the way with his own hand. Yes, and his will was that that day should be observed, with the intention that its remembrance should be more certain.

And for the same cause he pointed out the month that answers to March or April. Not directly to either one, however, because we cannot make a certain report of the months of the

Jews to compare them to ours. The reason for it is that they had their months intermingled one with another, because they took them according to the moon so that they are interlaced together. This month was therefore sometimes sooner and sometimes later, and was named in Hebrew *Abib*, which signifies an ear of corn, when it begins to shoot forth in the beginning. Not when the ears of corn are full ripe, but when the corn newly begins to grow. Indeed, the time of it imports nothing, but it did serve greatly to the instruction of the people because the setting of it made them behold the matter the more presently. God's putting of them in remembrance of it was such as they could not but know the meaning whereby their fathers were brought out of the land of Egypt. And the very night itself was marked to the end that they should consider how God had delivered them from the bondage of Pharaoh. On the other side, had the month been marked at the pleasure of men, they would have thought it might well have been changed for the convenience of the people. But God commanded it to be kept, to the end that they would know he would have no part in the changing of his ordinance, nor any attempt of man to alter it.

And now we have to mark in effect that by the ordaining of the Passover day God meant to set down a memorial of his work among his people that they might acknowledge his grace in delivering them out of the land of Egypt after that fashion, and that their children might know that that was the means whereby they were come into the inheritance that had been promised them. Nevertheless, it was not God's intent to be honored and served with a trifling ceremony, but his mind was that there should be teaching, that men might be edified by it, and that the Jews might know that God's calling of them to himself was to be served by them as their redeemer and father. And, therefore, he would not have the paschal lamb eaten by unholy and unbelieving people; but that it should be given to only as such were circumcised, and were already of the body of the Church. And seeing it so, we must have instruction annexed to lead us unto him. And for as much as we have the true Passover in our Lord Jesus Christ, as shall be declared tomorrow, we must nowadays step further. And although we do not have the old ceremony, yet let us hold fast the truth thereof, which is brought us by the son of God, as it is declared unto us in these days by his Gospel.

Now let us fall down before the majesty of our good God with acknowledgement of our sins, praying him to make us to perceive in what state we were, when he vouchsafed to call us to him. So as he plucked us out of the gulf of death, we have now cause to glorify him, and to give ourselves over to his service all the time of our life. And for as much as he not only shows himself to be our father and savior in this transitory life, but also calls us to the everlasting inheritance of heaven; according to his choice of us before the creation of the world, let us tend always there, and be the more provoked to labor to that end, seeing that we have the help and remedies which he gives us, and that the badge is kept among us as he had commanded us by his word. That it may please him to grant this grace not only to us, but also to all people and nations of the earth.

General Index

Academy at Geneva 53–63
Alexandrian School 10
allegorical interpretation of Scripture 10–12
Amama, Sixtinus 75–6
Anjorrant, Jacob 74
Antiochene School 10
Aquinas, Thomas 11
Augustine of Hippo 10–11

Basel 14, 19–20
Battles, F. L. 59
 and Hugo, A. M. 14–15, 16–17
Beeke, J. R. 21, 23
Belgic Confession 70
Bérauld, François 55
Bertram, Corneille 63
Beza, Theodore
 on Calvin's study of Hebrew 14
 on Calvin's use of hermeneutics 9
 as Europe's best Bible scholar 72
 excellence in Greek 78
 leaves Lausanne and joins Academy 54–5
 opening convocation address at Academy 56–7
 on providential protection of Geneva 56
 on Wolmar 19

biblical interpretation *see* hermeneutics
biblical languages *see* Greek; Hebrew; Latin
Borgeaud, C. 55
Bourges 18
Bouwsma, W. J. 13, 22, 59
Bucer, Martin 37, 52
Budé, Gillaume 40, 46, 47, 48
Bullinger, Henry 69

Calvin's language skills
 assessment of 12–13, 77–8
 demonstrated in preaching from original texts 28–9
 Greek study 18–20, 40–2
 Hebrew study 13–17
 and his expectations of students 49
 and his instrumental linguistic legacy 78
 sight-reading Hebrew text in lectures 46
 use of Greek in commentaries 39–43
 use of Hebrew in commentaries 33–5, 38–9
Calvin's writings
 commentaries *see* commentaries of Calvin
 Ecclesiastical Ordinances of 1541 52–3
 Institutes of the Christian Religion 45, 60

letter to Duke of Somerset 26
letter to Immanuel Tremellius 54
sermons *see* sermons
Cambridge, Emmanuel College 62, 76–7
Capito, Wolfgang 14
Chevallier, Antoine 55, 63
Chevallier, Pierre 63
Chrysostom, John 10
Church offices 45–6, 52–3
 Academy training of pastor-scholars 60
 lapsed pastoral role in Reformed circles 81
 ministerial need of studying biblical languages 81–4
Colinaeus text 25, 42
Colladon, Nicolas 28, 46–7
Collège de France 14–15, 40
 Faculty of the Sorbonne's suit against professors 16
commentaries of Calvin
 closing prayer to commentary on Hosea 1:1-2 47–8
 Commentary on Second Corinthians 18–19
 etymological research used in 34–5
 extent of 31–3
 lectures as source for some 49
 use of Greek 39–43
 use of Hebrew 33–5, 38–9
 use of rabbinics 35–8
Crispin, Jean 46
Currid, John: *Genesis* 33–4

Danes, Pierre 14, 40
Denney, James 79
Diodati, Jean 63

Ecclesiastical Ordinances of 1541 52–3
Edinburgh, University of 62, 77
education
 at the Academy 57–60, 74–5
 Calvin's lectures 46–9
 Farel's school in Geneva 51–2
 legacy and influence of the Academy 61–3, 74–7
 modern disregard of biblical languages in pastoral education 79–81
 study of biblical languages *see* Greek; Hebrew
Emmanuel College, Cambridge 62, 76–7
Erasmus 17, 42, 66
Erdos, K. 25

Estienne, Henri 40
etymology 34–5

Farel, Guillaume 51–2
Francis I, king of France 14, 40
Fuhrmann, P. T. 13, 23

Gamble, R. C. 61
Geneva
 the Academy 53–63
 adoption of the Reformation 51–2
 Beza on plots against, and providential protection of 56
 Calvin's expulsion, 1538 52
 Calvin's return to, 1541 52
 as centre of biblical textual scholarship 72
Genevan church 52–3
 'Marian' refugees arrive from England 71–2
 teaching ministry in 21–2, 46
Geneva Bible 71–4
Gerstner, J. H. 21, 23
Golding, Arthur 85–6
Great Bible of 1539 72, 73
Greek
 Calvin's study of 18–20, 40–2
 ministerial need of studying 81–4
 monastic hostility towards study of 65–6
 Septuagint (LXX) 24, 35
 taught at the Academy 58–9, 74–5
 texts probably used by Calvin 24–5, 41–2
 use in commentaries 39–43
Grynaeus, Simon 14, 19–20

Hafemann, S. 81, 82
Hall, Basil 77
Harbison, E. Harris 61
Hebrew
 Calvin's sight-reading Hebrew text in lectures 46
 Calvin's study of 13–17
 European hostility towards study of 16–17, 65–6
 ministerial need of studying 81–4
 taught at the Academy 58–60, 74–5
 texts probably used by Calvin for preaching 24
 use in Calvin's commentaries 33–5, 38–9
Helvetic Confession, Second 71

Henderson, Edward 77
hermeneutics
 Calvin's denunciation of allegory 12
 Calvin's grammatical-historical exegesis 9–10
 in Genesis 1–11 33–5, 39
 and God's authorship of original texts 70–1, 82
 need of solid knowledge of Greek and Hebrew for 12, 49, 69–70
 pre-Reformation use of allegory 10–11
 and translation of Psalm 22:16b 36
 use of rabbinics 35–8
 Zwingli's views on importance of knowledge of Hebrew for 68–9
Hugh of St. Victor 11
Hunter, A. M. 9, 12–13

inspiration and authority of Scripture 70–1, 82
Institutes of the Christian Religion 45, 60

James I 73–4
Jerome's translation of the Bible (Vulgate) 24, 34, 35, 42, 65, 66
John Chrysostom 10
Johnson, D. E. 82

Knox, John 78

Latin
 Augustine's belief in inspiration of Old Latin translation of the Bible 10–11
 Calvin's commentaries in 32
 Calvin's lectures in 46, 48, 49
 Jerome's translation of the Bible (Vulgate) 24, 34, 35, 42, 65, 66
 taught at the Academy 57, 58, 59
Lausanne 54
lectures 46–9
Leges Academiae Genevensis 56
Leiden, University of 62, 75–6
Lloyd Jones, G. 55, 57, 65, 73
Luther, Martin 45, 61, 66–7, 81

Mary Tudor 71
Melanchthon, Philipp 20, 68
Mildmay, Sir Walter 76
Münster, Sebastian 15
 Hebrew Bible 24

Nicoll, William Robertson 79–80

Origen 10
Orléans 18

Parker, T. H. L. 22
 on Calvin's lectures 49
 on French commentary on Joshua 32
 on Greek texts used by Calvin 25, 42
pastoral office
 Calvin's concern for an educated pastorate 77, 78
 distinguished from teaching office 45
 neglect and need of biblical language skills in 81–4
 training for 53, 60
prayer 46, 47–8
preaching
 Calvin's exegetical method 21–4
 Calvin's style 24–8
 extemporary 25–6
 Greek texts probably used by Calvin 24–5, 41–2
 from Hebrew and Greek testaments 28–9
 Hebrew texts probably used by Calvin 24
 modern disregard of biblical languages 79–81
 use of extrabiblical texts 24
Puckett, D. L. 36, 77

rabbinics 35–8
Raguenier, Denis 25, 27
Rebitté, D. 39–40
Reformation
 advanced by Geneva Bible 72
 Calvin's influence on reformed exegetes 37
 commitment to study of biblical languages 66–71, 83–4
 confessions 70–1, 82
 emphasis on literal interpretation of biblical texts 11–12
 Geneva's adoption of 51–2
 modern loss of Reformation's linguistic heritage 79–81
 Protestant persecution under Mary Tudor 71
Reuchlin, Johann 66, 67
Rohls, J. 70
Roset, Michel 56

Scaliger, Joseph 26
Schaff, Philip 13, 20

scriptural authority and inspiration 70-1, 82
Septuagint (LXX) 24, 35
sermons
    Calvin's sermon on Deuteronomy 16:1-4 85–102
    Calvin's view of importance of 21
    length of 27
    Raguenier's work as amanuensis 25, 27
    see also preaching
Servetus, Michael 37–8
Sheppard, G. T. 72
Simon, Richard 12
Sorbonne, Faculty of the 16
Stephanus text 25, 42
Strassburg 15, 52, 56
Sturm, J. 56

Tagaut, Jean 55
teaching office 45–6
    Calvin's lectures 46–9

textual criticism 41, 42
Theodore of Mopsuestia 10
Thomas Aquinas 11

Vatable, François 14, 15
Vulgate (Jerome's Latin translation of the Bible) 24, 34, 35, 42, 65, 66

Walker, W. 53, 58, 61–2
Waltke, B. K. 82
Watson, Richard 80
Westcott, B. F. 73
Westminster Confession 70–1, 82
Whittingham, William 72
Wolmar, Melchior 18–19

Zachman, R. C. 24, 27n30
Zwingli, Ulrich 68–9

Other books of interest from Christian Focus Publications

Why Do I Suffer?
Suffering and the Sovereignty of God
John Currid

Why *does* God allow suffering?

It's a question that, in one form or another rears its ugly head time and again. Whether it comes from someone who has just lost a loved one, been diagnosed with an incurable illness or even just surveyed the plight of poor in the third world. Every terrorist attack or world disaster raises the question – Where was God in this?

The question is one that has dogged Christians down the ages. A number of answers have been offered – and indeed all worldviews attempt their own response. John Currid brings Biblical teaching to bear. God does work in suffering, he is not a worried observer unwilling or unable to intervene, rather he has a purpose at work and is in control.

As Abraham said "Shall not the Judge of all the Earth do right?"

Grasping that truth will help us as we face the future and ensure that when we are next faced with that most tricky of questions we will know where to begin.

John Currid is Carl McMurray Professor of Old Testament at Reformed Theological Seminary, Jackson, Mississippi. He is a prolific author whose books include well received, multi-volume commentaries on Genesis, Exodus and soon Leviticus.

ISBN 1 85792 954 3

Calvin's teaching on Job
Proclaiming the Incomprehensible God
Derek Thomas

The book of Job stands at the core of one of the most complicated problems of life, the interaction between divine sovereignty and human responsibility. The implications for a world of suffering and injustice is one that has provoked much torutred discussion. It also lies at the heart of the World's accusation to the church 'If God is sovereign why doesn't he sort this mess out?'

In Job we see a previously blessed believer who is faced with tremendous suffering, it does not make for a neat story with simple applications. This is why the book of Job is often avoided by preachers - it is to difficult a book when simpler, more comfortable, options are available.

But the reality is that the issues Job faced are all issues that Christians will struggle with. Preachers must be willing to bring the Biblical teaching on them in Job to their congregations.

Although one of the church's most influential theologians Calvin was primarily a preacher. His sermons on Job are of interest on a number of levels, as a model for preacher today, for what they reveal of Calvin's approach to human suffering and to give answers to a world that lacks satisfying answers.

> 'Calvin's Sermons on Job are a fascinating part of his voluminous heritage. Derek Thomas's able exposition guides us through some of the key issues raised by the text. His work contains valuable lessons both for the understanding of Calvin and for the task of the preacher today.'
> Anthony N. S. Lane
> London Bible College

Dr. Derek Thomas is John E. Richards Professor of Practical and Systematic Theology at the Reformed Theological Seminary in Jackson, Mississippi.

ISBN 1 85792 922 5

Calvin and the Sabbath
The Controversy of applying the Fourth Commandment
Richard Gaffin

Sabbath, Sunday or The Lord's Day? Is there a difference? Is this a new argument?

If Sunday is the Sabbath then the Christian church is living in wholesale disregard to the will of God and is under his condemnation. If the Sabbath is no longer binding on the Christian then sections of the church are guilty of Pharisaism and are adding extra rules to Christ's teaching.

What was Calvin's viewpoint?

Galvin is still revered as one of the foremost developers of Christian doctrine. More than any other reformer Calvin sought to understand the great doctrines of Christianity and apply them to everyday living.

Richard Gaffin is the Professor of Biblical and Systematic Theology at Westminster Seminary. He has studied the extant writings of Calvin and produced a comprehensive understanding of his view of the Sabbath - you may be surprised at his findings!

Not only does Gaffin show what Calvin thought, he also critiques his conclusions and compares them to other reformers and confessional statements of the period.

This makes a fascinating study of the theology of the reformation and a valuable addition to Calvin studies.

Richard Gaffin is Professor of Biblical and Systematic Theology at Westminster Theological Seminary, Philadelphia.

ISBN 1 85792 3766

Calvin and the Atonement
What the renowned pastor and teacher said about the cross of Christ
Robert A Peterson Sr.

John Calvin had a profound understanding of the atoning work of Christ. His writings are still one of the major sources scholars and others rely on to give insight into what was accomplished by Jesus on the cross.

In this book Robert Peterson first examines what Calvin says regarding the love of God, the Incarnation, and Christ's offices of prophet, priest and king. He goes on to consider Calvin's comments on other aspects of Christ's work: he is the second Adam, the victor, the substitute, the sacrifice and the example.

'Calvin dealt with Christ's saving ministry, as with all other biblical themes, in a different way.... Dr. Peterson's monograph lays out the elements of this synthesis in a way that Calvin himself would certainly have approved. The task has not been tackled in print before in so adequate a manner, and this essay is something of a milestone. I commend it heartily, both as a fine contribution to modern Calvin studies and as a worthy presentation of insights into a central theme of scripture from one of the greatest Bible expositors of all time.'

J. I. Packer, Regent College, Vancouver

'Rather than fall into the trap of insisting on one 'theory' of the atonement, John Calvin recognised that the biblical teaching presents us with a multi-faceted jewel. His brilliant exposition stressed the many-sidedness and the profundity of the work of Christ. The great strength of Dr Robert Peterson's work lies in his grasps of Calvin's biblical vision and the clarity and enthusiasm with which he expounds it. Sixteen years after its first publication this revised edition of Calvin and the Atonement will be welcomed by a new generation of readers.'

Sinclair B Ferguson

Robert A Peterson Sr. is on the faculty of Covenant Seminary in St. Louis. He has also written on the biblical nature of hell and the major themes of the gospel of John.

ISBN 1 85792 377 4

Christian Focus Publications
publishes books for all ages

Our mission statement –

STAYING FAITHFUL
In dependence upon God we seek to help make His infallible Word, the Bible, relevant. Our aim is to ensure that the Lord Jesus Christ is presented as the only hope to obtain forgiveness of sin, live a useful life and look forward to heaven with Him.

REACHING OUT
Christ's last command requires us to reach out to our world with His gospel. We seek to help fulfil that by publishing books that point people towards Jesus and help them develop a Christ-like maturity. We aim to equip all levels of readers for life, work, ministry and mission.

Books in our adult range are published in three imprints.
Christian Focus contains popular works including biographies, commentaries, basic doctrine and Christian living. Our children's books are also published in this imprint.
Mentor focuses on books written at a level suitable for Bible College and seminary students, pastors, and other serious readers. The imprint includes commentaries, doctrinal studies, examination of current issues and church history.
Christian Heritage contains classic writings from the past.

Christian Focus Publications, Ltd
Geanies House, Fearn,
Ross-shire, IV20 1TW, Scotland, United Kingdom
info@christianfocus.com

Our titles are available from quality bookstores and
www.christianfocus.com